HIS GLORY,
HIS WAY

R OB S CHLEIDER

ISBN: 978-1-5356-0618-9

Dedications

God puts people in our path to not only grow us and complete us, but to give us the joy of loving others and being loved by others.

To Susan, my wife of forty-three years, who led me to the Lord with her zeal for living through Him. Thanks for loving the Lord with all your heart, soul, and mind. Thank you.

To our children, Rob and Callie, who have given us the greatest joy and privilege on earth of being your parents. We will always remember the love we had for you when we first saw you in the delivery room. A love only God can give, and a love that has grown each day with tremendous respect, honor, and admiration. We thank you.

To our children through marriage, Tony Varisco IV and Katie Hamilton Schleider, who were the answer to over twenty-five years of praying. We thank you.

To our grandkids: Quinn, Reid, Vonn, Tony, and Elle. Thanks for keeping us young with your endless enthusiasm. We pray daily that each of you receive Jesus into your heart as Lord and Savior. We thank you.

To our parents in heaven with the Lord, Bob and Ann Schleider, and Jimmie Cummings, who loved us, taught us, and sacrificed so much for us. We thank you.

To my mother-in-law, Georgia Cummings (GiGi), thanks for your prayers, witness and daily reflection of Christ. We thank you.

To my brother, Reg, the most thoughtful and giving person I know. Thanks for always being there for me. We thank you.

To my sister-in-law, Betty Milburn, thanks for the support and encouragement. We thank you.

To my "Bible Study" group, Mike Gentry, Chip Howard, David Decker, Chuck Moreau, and Scott Sigle, thanks for being men of character, men of prayer, and men of God. We thank you.

To Dwight Edwards, author of several books, and pastor of WatersEdge Community Church in Houston, Texas, thanks for your book, *Revolution Within*, the book God used to touch my heart regarding the purpose for our creation, His Glory. We thank you.

To the late H. Baily Stone Jr. and Dr. Buckner Fanning, thanks for your sermons from the heart of God that helped me to better understand the love and grace of God. We thank you.

To Laurie Carlton, Kiersten Bastow, and Garrison White at Chick-fil-A, thanks for making me feel so special while I wrote so much of the book in your restaurant. Your smiles while you said, "Good morning, Rob," always made my day. We thank you.

To Dr. Curtis Garrett, thanks for always believing in me and providing a Christ-like light in times of darkness. Thanks also for your oral surgeon skills, I never felt a thing. I thank you.

To Dr. Mario Lammoglia, thanks for being my cardiologist and friend, God used you to save my life twice. We thank you. We thank you.

To Ray Court, thanks for your friendship and making me laugh. We thank you.

To the many others God used to bring me closer to Him. We thank you.

Contents

Foreword

ISAIAH **43:7** "EVERYONE WHO IS called by my name, whom I created for my Glory…"

JOHN **17:4** "I HAVE BROUGHT you Glory on earth by completing the work you gave me to do."

Do you want God to bless you in the path of your preference, or do you seek to Glorify God in the path of His choosing? Is your prayer life filled with the word "bless"? "Lord, "bless me," "bless my health," "bless my family," "bless my finances," "bless my path," "bless this," "bless that," …." Or does the word "Glorify" and "Glory" echo over and over in your prayers? Does the Lord hear, "Please direct me in the path for your greatest Glory," "Please Glorify yourself through me today," "Please Glorify yourself through my family, my wife, my children, my grandchildren," or "Lord, I don't know why this happened and you know how much I'm hurting, but please Glorify your name through it all?"

The word "bless" isn't the problem; it's the pronouns afterward, me or my that can shift the attention to us and not Him. Is it about you? No. Is it about me? Certainly not. It's about Him. It's about His Glory. It's about His way in receiving that Glory. His Glory, His way.

His Glory, His Tree

LUKE 2:40 "AND THE CHILD grew and became strong; he was filled with wisdom, and the grace of God was upon Him."

LUKE 2:52 "AND JESUS GREW in wisdom and stature, and in favor with God and men."

MATTHEW 13:55A "ISN'T THIS THE carpenter's son?"

As Jesus grew, "the grace of God was upon Him." Upon Him as He grew up in Nazareth. Upon Him as Mary and Joseph fed Him, clothed Him, and nurtured Him. Upon Him as He learned about wood in His father's carpenter shop. Upon Him as He "grew in stature." Upon Him as He grew in wisdom. Upon Him as He grew "in favor with God and man." Upon Him as He read God's word. Upon Him as He prayed. Upon Him as He grew in understanding and knowledge.

But just as God was nurturing His son in His growth, at the same time He was nurturing a tree in its growth, a tree that would one day hold His son at Calvary. God providing nourishment for both His son and His tree.

Both growing in stature. Both growing strong. One having the strength to hold Him there. One having the love to stay there. One bearing the body of His son. One bearing the sins of all mankind. One planted by God. One sent by God. One cut by man. One crucified by man. The one cut would come down. The One crucified wouldn't stay down. The one cut would die. The One crucified would also die, but this One would be raised to bring God His greatest Glory. "Father, the time has come, Glorify your Son." (John 17:1)

It is highly unlikely that God is now providing nourishment for a tree that will one day be strong enough to hold you as you are being crucified. However, it is highly likely that God has provided, is now providing, or will provide nourishment for a person that has, is, or will bring you disappointment, trouble, or pain.

The foreman stood up and told the judge that the jury was unanimous in awarding me $245,000 for the fraud and misrepresentation of facts the bank had used in its dealings with me. Later, the foreman told me that he would have awarded me millions of dollars if he could have legally done so, because he and the other jurors were outraged regarding the bank's actions and deception. I didn't want to go down this road, but the bank had forced my hand. And now there was justice, but short-lived justice.

Several months later the appellate court overturned the twelve jurors' decision and awarded the bank $225,000. I was devastated. Then I got angry. Angry with the bank. Angry with the court system. But my real anger was toward God. I called Him names. I called Him a liar. I told Him that He either blinked or didn't care about me. I held up my fist and told him to "stick it." I told Him if this was the way He treated His children, then He should be put in jail for child abuse. I yelled at Him to leave me alone because His so-called love for me was killing me. My thoughts were shameful, but I felt no shame, only anger and betrayal.

So I left to the "far country." My address didn't change, my location stayed the same, but I left Him. Sadly, I stayed in the far country for several years, all the while justifying my anger for His "child abuse." Then, I came to my senses. I was tired of fighting Him. I could no longer hold up my fist in anger. I was completely emptied with nothing left in me.

On my knees, I asked the very God whom I had called horrible names and levied terrible accusations if I could come back home. I didn't think I had the right to ask Him this, but I still believed His forgiveness was greater than my sin, and His open arms of love were greater than my fists of anger.

He lovingly said in His own way, "Rob, I've been waiting for your return since the very day you walked out on me. You left me for the 'far country,' but you were always in My heart and in My thoughts. Of course you can come back home, but we need to get one thing settled or else you will leave again and again. You were right in believing I created you to bring Me Glory, just like all of My creation. But what you failed to understand at the time was how I received my Glory through you was up to Me as well. If I allowed My Son, a perfect Son who lived in perfect obedience, to be crucified on a cross for My greatest Glory, then you are open season. Are we clear?

"I used that bank to grow you. But before I could grow you, I had to untangle some misguided beliefs you had picked up along the way. Beliefs that had taken deep root and had wrapped around your heart, squeezing My Spirit in you, a belief that your obedience entitled you to choose any fruit from my orchard of blessings. A belief that it was about My Glory, but in the way of your choosing, not Mine. A belief that your 'goodness' gave you, not Me, the right to choose the path for My Glory. I know it was painful, but I loved you too much to allow you to continue to suffocate in your beliefs and theology that sought 'your blessings over My Glory.'"

Alan Redpath once wrote, "When God sets forth to do an impossible task, He then seeks the willing heart through an impossible man, and then crushes him." Why the pain? Why the crushing? Does God get great joy in seeing us hurt, in pain, and in sorrow? No, but in His perfect love He knows we must first be emptied of self and crushed of all personal ambitions, desires, and pursuits so that His Glory can reflect through us.

Maybe the next time someone crosses your path that causes you pain and sorrow, think that possibly the Lord grew them in order to grow you, and a growing you grows His Glory.

His Glory. His Growing you.

His Glory, His Hands

ISAIAH **49:16** "SEE, I HAVE engraved you on the palms of my hand."

JOHN **20:27** "THEN HE SAID to Thomas, 'Put your finger here; see my hands.'"

JOHN **10:28** "...NO ONE CAN snatch them out of my hand."

JOHN **20:28** "...THOMAS SAID TO Him, 'My Lord and my God.'"

Our (my wife Susan and mine's) daughter, Callie, is beautiful in so many ways. In fact, I call her "gorgeous" more than her given name of Callie. But as beautiful as she is on the outside, it doesn't compare to her inward beauty of a heart and a spirit that both reflect the Lord and bring Him Glory day in and day out.

As a child, she was a bundle of energy, always asking questions like, "Does God snore?" Each and every day was a holiday. Each and every day was go, go, and go some more. Each and every day was full throttle, ninety to nothing. However, each and every day also had some form of mischievousness thrown in somewhere along the way. Unbound energy left unchecked could bring unwanted results at the most unwanted time. That was Callie. Get the picture?

Callie's seventh birthday was approaching, maybe a couple of weeks away. Susan had bought the perfect birthday invitations as she always did. She was sitting at the kitchen table with Callie addressing the invitations to those invited to her birthday party while I watched. They talked and laughed as Susan put that final personal touch on each envelope, and when finished said, "All done! I just need to buy some stamps and then I'll mail them." As I walked away, I looked back at Callie and saw that "look" I'd seen so many times before. That "look," which meant her mind was racing, which meant "sound the alarm, all hands on deck."

The next morning I took Callie and our son, Robby, to school. On a normal day, Callie would do all the talking, and Robby and I would do all the listening. But not this day. This day, not a word was said, although I thought I heard Robby whisper a couple of times, "Callie, don't do that." But I passed it on as just my imagination, my angels are just quiet today.

When we arrived at their school, I stopped the car and opened the back doors to let them out of their car seats. I unbuckled Robby first, hugged him, told him I loved him, and off he went.

I then went around the car to unbuckle Callie from her car seat. As I was doing so, she said with a big smile on her face and a loud excited voice, "Daddy, look at my hands." I did so and saw that they were both covered in blue ink, lots and lots of blue ink. The unusual quietness had now been explained and my concern about the "look" the night before had now become a fulfilled prophecy.

"Callie, why did you draw on your hands?" I asked.

"Daddy, I didn't draw anything. Look, my hands are invitations. I wrote each name of everyone invited to my birthday party on my hands.

See? I'm going to go up to each person today that is invited, show them my hands with their name on them, and tell them, 'You're invited. Your name is written on my hand.' Tell Mom she doesn't need to buy stamps now. She will be thrilled."

I thought, she would only be thrilled if I told her, because this could be trouble for me. I could just hear Susan saying, "Rob, don't you know by now that when Callie is quiet, either she is sick or into something?"

Obviously, not yet.

Then I began to think, "handwritten invitations," "look at my hands," and "your name is written on my hand." Through Callie's hands, God had made the scriptures come alive. Just as Callie had used her hands as her own "personal invitation list," God used the nail-scarred hands of His Son for His own "personal invitation list."

Then the words of Isaiah 49:16 became ever so clear, so vivid. "See I have engraved you on the palms of my hands." On the hands of Jesus at Calvary, on the cross, my name, your name, His "personalized invitation list" to eternity for all who accept His invitation by faith. Invitations not written on the hands of a little girl with a blue ink pen, but engraved on the hands of the body of God with crimson-stained spikes.

And then the words of Jesus, "no one can snatch them out of my hand," became all so clear. We aren't an object held in the hand of God but a name engraved in the very body of God. No formal invitations, just personalized hands. No stamps, just engraved hands.

Engraved hands that Jesus showed to Thomas and said, "See my hands."

And after looking at His hands and touching His side, Thomas said, "My Lord and My God." The only person in the New Testament to call Jesus "God."

Does the Lord want to show us, like He did Thomas, a closer look at His hands? Not a casual glance, but a sustained look. Should the One whose hands bear our name, and bearing all sins in that name, engraved by crimson-stained spikes, receive from us a life devoted for His Glory?

Should our hands bear resemblance to His hands? Hands cupped in prayer? Hands of sacrifice? Hands willing to be engraved by the will of God? Hands submitted to the Glory of God? And finally, is there someone whose name is engraved in the hands of God for all eternity because that someone first saw our hands engraved with the love of God as we were seeking to bring Glory to God?

His Glory. His hands. Our hands.

His Glory, His Autobiography

MATTHEW 3:16, 17 "As soon as Jesus was baptized, He went up out of the water. At that moment heaven was opened, and He saw the Spirit of God descending like a dove and lighting on Him. And a voice from heaven said, 'This is my Son, whom I love; with Him I am well pleased.'"

MATTHEW 4:1-10 "THEN JESUS WAS led by the Spirit into the desert to be tempted [tested] by the devil. After fasting forty days and forty nights, He was hungry. The tempter came to Him and said, 'If you are the Son of God, tell these stones to become bread.'

"Jesus answered, 'It is written: "man does not live on bread alone, but on every word that comes from the mouth of God."' (Deuteronomy 8:3)

"Then the devil took Him to the holy city and had Him stand on the highest point of the temple. 'If you are the Son of God,' he said, 'throw yourself down. For it is written: "He will command His angels concerning you, and they will lift you up in their hands, so that you will not strike your foot against a stone.'" (Psalm 91:11, 12)

"Jesus answered him, 'It is also written: "Do not put the Lord your God to the test."' (Deuteronomy 6:16)

"Again, the devil took Him to a very high mountain and showed Him all the kingdoms of the world and their splendor. 'All this I will give you,' he said, 'if you will bow down and worship me.'

"Jesus said to him, 'Away from me, satan! For it is written: "worship the Lord your God, and serve Him only."'" (Deuteronomy 6:13)

Mark 1:13 "And He was in the desert forty days being tempted [tested] by satan. He was with the wild animals and angels attended Him."

Matthew 27:39, 40, 41 "Those who passed by hurled insults at Him, shaking their heads and saying, 'You who are going to destroy this temple and build it in three days, save yourself! Come down from the cross if you are the son of God.'

"In the same way the chief priests, the teachers of the law and the elders mocked Him."

Luke 23:36 "The soldiers also came up and mocked Him."

Luke 23:39 "One of the criminals who hung there hurled insults at Him."

Matthew 26:53 "Do you think I cannot call on my Father, and he will at once put at my disposal more than twelve legions of angels?"

What would you write in your autobiography? Regardless of your age, what would you want others to know about you, and the things you believe to be of most importance? What would you want to share with your friends? Your classmates? Your brothers? Your sisters? Your children? Your grandkids? Your spouse? Your parents?

What about life lessons? Sure. Meaningful moments? Of course. Decisions made at the crossroads? You bet. Tremendous challenges? Yes. Great victories? Absolutely. What about a specific time of testing that laid the foundation for your life? A must. As you think about what would be important to you, let's look at what was important to our Lord, enough so that He made sure that "His autobiography" in the desert was part of the word of God for the world to know.

At His baptism, God spoke, saying, "This is my Son, whom I love; with Him I am well pleased." (Matthew 3:17) Shortly thereafter, Jesus would hear the voice of satan, questioning Him and commanding Him. From the dove to the devil. From the assurance of God to the questions of satan. From the voice of God to the voice of satan. From His baptism to His battleground.

After His baptism, Jesus was led by the Spirit of God into the desert to be tested by satan. Jesus, the Spirit of God, the angels, and satan. No one else. No disciples. No parents. No Mary. No Joseph. No brothers or sisters. No friends. No pastors. No counselors. No audience. No one taking notes. No one writing down what happened, what was said. No one.

This was His time, the time to begin His ministry, His three-year journey to the cross starting in the desert. This was His place, the desert, where satan would question His relationship with God not once, but twice, saying, "If you are the Son of God…" This was His place, the desert, where satan not once, but twice commanded Him. Once to "feed yourself," and then to "throw yourself." This was His time, His place where satan was saying, "Show them spectacular, show them sensational so they will not see you as a servant, as a Savior. Wow them with miracles so they will not worship you as Messiah. Turn their heads with splendor so they will not fix their eyes and hearts on you and the cross." This was His place, where satan promised to give Him what wasn't his to give.

We don't know much about the early years of Jesus, His childhood, His teen years, His early adult life. But we do know about the beginning of His ministry as He was tested by the devil in the desert. We do know He told some, or all, of His disciples about this time because Matthew, Mark, and Luke wrote about it, and they weren't there. We do know He wanted this testing in His life, this time in the desert, His "autobiography" in His word for you and me to read. But why? Why was it so important for Him and for us?

By IQ standards, my dad was a genius. Add common sense, Godly wisdom, the gift of teaching, and leadership qualities to a servant's heart and you have a man that had two different cities (College Station, Texas, and Wichita Falls, Texas) name a day in his honor, "Bob Schleider Day".

Starting in junior high school, he taught me and reminded me several times throughout my life the importance of making life's most important decisions on your knees, alone with God. He told me, "You must decide what you believe in, what is important to you, and whom you will serve. What is right and what is wrong. What you will do and not do. What you will be and not be. What will define you. Will honesty? Will integrity? Will character? Will God's word? Will service? What temptations will you say no to when they come knocking? Cheating? Lying? Drinking? Drugs? Compromise?" And then he added, "Son, when those temptations and tests come knocking, and they will, if you haven't already decided on your knees before God to say "no," then it will be too late once you answer the door."

He would always close with a positive and encouraging word. "Most battles are won before they are ever fought [he was in the Marine Corps], battles won by planning and preparation, conviction and courage. Be prepared to say no. Plan on the tests, the temptations, and have the courage to do what is right with conviction and the perseverance to stay right."

While on the cross, the chief priests, the teachers of the law, the elders, those crucified with Him, and those passing by all mocked Him by saying, "Come down from the cross if you are the Son of God." The soldiers also mocked Him, saying, "If you are the King of the Jews, save yourself." Mocking Him to "free" Himself.

I just wonder if Jesus looked down at that soldier telling Him to "come down and free Yourself," realizing He had heard that same voice once before in the desert, telling Him to "feed" Himself. The devil's first shot in the desert to "feed Himself" and his last shot at Calvary to "free Himself." Jesus says in Matthew 26:53 that He could call on His Father and at once twelve legions (up to 144,000) of angels would be by His side. Could it be that His decision to not call on the angels to "free Himself" was made three years earlier in the desert where He decided who He would worship, who He would serve, and how He would use His powers only to bring Glory to God, not for Himself?

Was His triumph at Calvary a result of His victory in the desert? Did God's greatest Glory coming on a cross come because of the victories of Jesus in the desert? Were all those angels waiting anxiously for the call that never came?

Will God receive His greatest Glory through us because of decisions we once made in prayer, on our knees, "in the desert," which later became victories in the Lord for others to see?

Decisions made before the tests came.

Decisions made before the temptations knocked.

Decisions made before the questions were asked.

Decisions made before the choices were presented.

Decisions made before the crossroads were visible.

Decisions made then, which makes your autobiography now, a reflection of His Glory.

Decisions made now, which will make your autobiography later, a reflection of His Glory.

His Glory. His autobiography. Your autobiography.

His Glory, His "Two Words"

MARK 16:7 "BUT GO, TELL his disciples and Peter."

LUKE 24:34 "IT IS TRUE. The Lord has risen and has appeared to Simon."

ACTS 4:4 "BUT MANY WHO heard the message believed, and the number of men grew to about five thousand."

LUKE 22:32 "…AND WHEN YOU have turned back, strengthen your brothers."

The Bible only sheds light to bring Glory to One, that being Jesus. All others have invisible faults, weaknesses, and sins that are revealed openly for the world to see. We read about "Fearful Abraham," "Doubting Thomas," "Persecuting Paul," and "Denying Peter."

Peter, he's the one who said he would never deny Jesus, but he did, and he did, and he did. He's the one who said he would stand by His side, but he didn't. He's the one whose chin was dragging on the ground.

He's the one the angel told the woman at the tomb, "But go, tell his disciples and Peter."

"And Peter." Two words. Just two. "And Peter." Why didn't the angel just say, "Go and tell the disciples?" He was one of them, one of the eleven, so why single him out? Why add, "and Peter"?

Sometimes those that charge the hardest, fall the deepest. Sometimes those that fall the deepest need more words of encouragement, and sometimes just two words will do, "and Peter." Do you think it ever crossed Peter's mind that he was capable of denying the Lord three times and hearing the cock crow? Others yes, but him, never. Do you think Peter got so low and down on himself that he entertained thoughts of packing up his stuff, loading up the boat, and sailing off to a distant port to get as far away from his failures as possible? Do you think he kept thinking back to the first words Jesus told him, "You are Simon, son of John. You will be called Cephas, which when translated is Peter which means rock. (John 1:42) And then thinking, "Some rock I am. I'm a rock of denial. I'm a rock of failure."

Can you identify with Peter? Ever make a promise and not keep it? Ever make a commitment to the Lord and not keep it? Ever let a loved one down? Ever let the Lord down? Ever make a vow and not keep it? Ever fail? Ever want to pack up, leave, and start over? Ever had your head down, your chin dragging on the ground?

I'm twelve years old and pitching in a Little League All Star game against a neighboring town. The park is filled with fans from both sides, it's the last inning and we are ahead 2 to 1. There are two outs and I'm thinking, "One more out, just one more, and we win." Our manager comes out to the mound and says, "Rob, you have a runner on second. First base is open. Do you want to pitch to "him" or walk "him?" "Him" was known as "Big Joe" and resembled Goliath to this little David. I told our manager, "I want to pitch to 'him.'" He said, "Okay, he's all yours."

I (David) threw him (Goliath) my best fastball, and he promptly hit it over the flagpole in centerfield for a homerun to win the game for them. Their crowd went crazy. Our crowd went quiet. I went numb.

The game is over. Our season is over and I remember all so well thinking, "You let your team down, your town down, you let everybody down." I come out of the gate leading to the stands with head down and tears a flowing. Then, out of nowhere, I feel "two fingers" lift my chin up and I see my dad with the biggest smile on his face that I had ever seen. There was no time to ask him, "Why the smile?" No time to tell him, "Don't you understand, I lost the game for us? I'm a loser. I'm a failure."

He says with that smile, "Son, you gave it your very best. You chose to face "Big Joe" and I've never been more proud of you than I am right now." Two fingers. It just took *two fingers* to lift my chin up to see a father's smiling face and hear words of encouragement that would stay with me forever.

My dad saw through the home run, through the loss, through the failure to see me through God's eyes and heart. I failed, but he didn't see a failure. I lost, but he didn't see a loser. His "two fingers," his smile and his words were forever etched in my heart because it showed that his love for me was not performance based, not based on wins or losses, victories or defeats, or any other condition. Just love. Pure, unconditional love. That same love the Lord has for us. The same love the Lord had for Peter.

Five years later, in May of 1969, at the age of seventeen, I signed a professional baseball contract with the Montreal Expos organization in the National League. There was only one line at the bottom of the contract for one person to sign. I signed it, but I knew there should have been "two fingerprints" by my signature, the "two fingerprints" of those "two fingers" that lifted my chin up, the "two fingers" of a loving father who saw through me with God's heart. And yes, he had the same exact smile on his face watching me sign that contract as he did when he lifted up my chin with his "two fingers."

Maybe because of the impact my dad's "two fingers" had on me, I can see the impact "two words" could have had on Peter. "And Peter." Can you imagine the conversation the messenger had with Peter?

Messenger: "'Peter,' he said, 'Go tell his disciples and Peter.'" Peter: "He said 'And Peter?' You're sure."

Messenger: "Yes. He said, 'And Peter.'" Peter: "My name. He said my name?" Messenger: "Yes, your name. 'And Peter.'"

Can't you just see Peter starting to unpack his boat? Can't you just see the gleam come back into his eyes, the confidence coming back into his voice, the fire coming back into his spirit? Can't you just see that chin being lifted up with "two words," and that life so devastated by failure become so alive with confident hope and expectation?

This story would lose all meaning if it were just about Peter then, because it is also a story about you and me today. God's word is true and timeless.

He continues to send messages to us to keep our chins up so we can always see the cross. He may use "two words" sent by a messenger, "two fingers" from the hand of a caring father, a text or telephone call, a mother's touch, a friend's companionship, or a pastor's sermon, but they are all sent from the heart of a loving God. A loving God, sending words of encouragement to us that have failed Him, failed others, and failed ourselves.

But that's not the end of the story. Far from it. His words of encouragement are meant for so much more than to lift our chins up. He sends His messengers to us, His words to us, His belief in us, and pursues us, to bring Him Glory.

God brought Peter back to bring Him Glory. Maybe God knew two words, "and Peter," would turn Peter back into the rock He said he would become, that rock which led five thousand men to become believers through his preaching (Acts 4:4), bringing God Glory.

We have a loving Father who lifts up our chins, lifts up our spirits to lift Him in Glory. God is seeking to bring you and me back to bring Him Glory. How he chooses to bring us back is not the issue, but why?

He brings us back to bring Him Glory, and then once back sends us out (like Peter) to bring others back, to bring Him Glory.

His Glory. His "two words." His "two fingers."

His Glory, His Timing

JOHN 11:4 "WHEN HE HEARD this, Jesus said, 'This sickness will not end in death. No, it is for God's Glory so that God's Son may be Glorified through it.'"

JOHN 11:6 "YET, WHEN HE heard that Lazarus was sick, He stayed where He was two more days."

We all know the story. Jesus is away. Lazarus, a close friend, becomes very sick. Jesus hears of his sickness, rushes back to Bethany and heals Lazarus from his illness. All is now well. Mary and Martha are grateful and say to Jesus, "Thanks for coming right away when we asked you and healing our brother. No telling what might have happened had you not rushed down here." So the story ends. All is now well in Bethany. No tears. No crying. No one dies. No one saying, "If you had been here, my brother would not have died." No funeral to attend. But then again, no one would have seen God's Glory. No one would have heard Jesus say, "I am the resurrection and the life. He who believes in me will live even though he dies, and whoever lives and believes in me will never die." (John 11:25) And no one would have seen Lazarus come out of a tomb, his home for four days. You're right, the scriptures tell us of a different story, a true one.

Lazarus is sick. Lazarus is dying. His sisters, Mary and Martha, send word to Jesus. "Lord, the one you love is sick." (John 11:3) His good friend Lazarus is going down quickly and needs immediate attention. Yet, Jesus stays where He is two more days after hearing the news. Lazarus dies. Lazarus is placed in a tomb wrapped in grave clothes.

After waiting two days, Jesus makes His way to Bethany, the village where Mary, Martha, and Lazarus lived. No rush. No urgency. When He does arrive, He is greeted by Martha and Mary, both saying to Him, "If you had been here, my brother would not have died." (John 11:21) Both in tears. Both question Him. Both call Him out. You heard. You stayed. You delayed. Now he's dead.

Have you ever questioned the Lord? His timing? His goodness? His care? His concern? Have you ever called Him out? Ever wondered, "Where is He?" Ever said, "Had you come when I called, when I asked, this wouldn't have happened"?

Being called out, does the Lord now call them out? Does He chide them for daring to question Him? His timing? His care? His love? No, no calling out, but He does cry with them. No calling, just tears. No calling, just compassion. He does, however, call Lazarus out. "Take away the stone." (John 11:39) "Lazarus, come out." (John 11:43) "The dead man came out..." (John 11:44)

Maybe we need to ask the Lord Jesus to "take away the stones" in our lives so that we can better hear the voice of God. Maybe no more retreats, no more study books until we allow Him to remove a few stones. Or maybe He is calling us out, seeking to resurrect those parts of us that have died. Some dreams? Some beliefs? Some values? Some hopes? Some relationship? Some part of your marriage?

"Jesus said to them, 'Take off the grave clothes and let him go.'" (John 11:44) Lazarus was wrapped in grave clothes, but could it be that we are wrapped up in past failures, past sins, past disappointments, and past hurts? Or possibly we may think we have done something so bad, so horrible, that we now think we belong in our grave clothes? We deserve them, we reason, and now they are a comfortable fit.

Maybe He is not "calling you out" in the way you think you deserve. Could it be that He is not calling you out, but calling you back? Back to Him? Back to fellowship with Him? Back to oneness with Him?

God's timing is never off, always on. The One who created time is never going to be late. We may question Him and call Him out, but He never rushes or panics. Think about it. He could have rushed down to Bethany to heal Lazarus, but by staying two days He brought God Glory by raising him from the dead.

Healing him might have brought relief to Mary and Martha, but raising him from the dead brought Glory to God. Yes, sometimes God heals us and restores us when we are broken. But sometimes, like Lazarus, He waits until that sickness or brokenness runs its full course to become a place of resurrection in our lives. Could it be that God waits to resurrect that part of us that must die and not just heal that part of us we are so desperately trying to resuscitate? Maybe God, in all His love, knows that there are times when our desire to patch things up and mend things must come to an end so that resuscitation can begin, bringing a new testimony for all to see.

I remember a night about forty-six years ago as if it happened yesterday...the night my professional baseball career came to a painful end. Several months earlier I had pitched a good game only to wake up the following morning feeling like someone had stuck an ice pick in my shoulder. It made no sense at all. None. I went to bed feeling great and woke up with an arm, my pitching arm, that I couldn't move.

Back in 1970, there wasn't an MRI to give the doctors a clear diagnosis. So our trainer began treatments of hot and cold packs on my shoulder. One day heat, the next day ice. No throwing, just rest. After two months of treatment, the pain went away. Finally, I could throw again. My shoulder had been patched up and was mending well.

After a month of throwing on the side, it was time to pitch in a game. I was eager in one way, but reluctant in another way. There were still fresh memories of a night five years earlier when I had broken my elbow pitching in a game. Would my shoulder hold up? Would the patchwork and mending stay strong? Would something break again?

I was given a pitch count, no more than thirty pitches. The first inning went great, fourteen pitches and three strikeouts. My fears were gone and the memories forgotten as I walked to the dugout. "Hey Schleider, you're back," a buddy hollered. "Just like before," another teammate said as he patted me on the back.

I went out to throw my warm-up pitches before the second inning. As I threw my last warm-up pitch, something popped in my shoulder that brought some serious pain. But that physical pain didn't compare to the mental pain of knowing my baseball career was over. My dream, no more. My questions, many. My foundation, crumbled. The patch work, shattered.

At the time, I was as dead spiritually as Lazarus was dead physically. But God, in His mercy, grace, and love, called me out of "my tomb," my baseball career, to give me life in Him. Three years later, my wife Susan and my pastor, Bailey Stone, led me to accept Jesus Christ as my Lord and Savior. My arm still hurts at times, but that pain resurrects a special memory causing me to thank the Lord for "not patching me up" and "mending" a life that I was living without Him.

Can you imagine the testimony Lazarus had from that day forward? The fingers pointed at him. The talk directed around him. The reputation spreading about him. But I just wonder if that same finger pointing, that same talk, and that same kind of reputation would be spread around about us in our schools, towns, and neighborhoods if we were to allow God to remove the stones silencing His voice and the grave clothes that have bound us, so that we could come out, called by God, to live a life for His Glory?

His Glory. His divine watch.

His Glory, His Lack of Dignity

LUKE 15: 11-13, 17-24 "JESUS continued: 'There was a man who had two sons. The younger one said to his father, "Father, give me my share of the estate." So he divided his property between them.

"Not long after that, the younger son got together all he had, set off for a distant country and there squandered his wealth in wild living...

"When he came to his senses...I will set out and go back to my father and say to him: 'Father, I have sinned against heaven and against you. I am no longer worthy to be called your son; make me like one of your hired men.' So he got up and went to his father.

"But while he was still a long way off, his father saw him and was filled with compassion for him; he ran to his son, threw his arms around him and kissed him.

"The son said to him, 'Father, I have sinned against heaven and against you. I am no longer worthy to be called your son.'

"But the father said to his servants, 'Quick! Bring the best robe and put it on him. Put a ring on his finger and sandals on his feet. Bring the fattened calf and kill it. Let's have a feast and celebrate. For this son of mine was dead and is alive again; he was lost and is found.' So they began to celebrate."

The parable of the lost son and the loving father. A story that so reveals the heart of God, a heart of love, of forgiveness, and of grace. A heart seeking oneness with His children, even a wayward one. Especially a wayward one. A heart of compassion, lacking nothing except dignity.

Jesus tells the story of a father with two sons. The younger son goes to the father and tells him in so many words, "Give me my inheritance and now, so I can get out of this place." The father does so, probably with a bruised heart for what the son asked and for the direction he knew he was headed. It was not the son's to take, but the Father's to give.

So the son departs to a far country, full of money, full of answers, and full of himself. But it didn't take him long to lose it all, his money, his pride, and his answers. Coming to his senses, he decides to go back home with nothing but a prepared speech of repentance to give to his father. No excuses, no rationalizations, no reasons, just repentance.

Can't you just see the son, with head down, going over and over his prepared speech of what he was going to tell his father. Maybe with tears in his eyes. Maybe with doubts of his father's response. Maybe with thoughts of his father's rejection. Maybe with worries of his future if his father won't take him back. And maybe not knowing the difference between what a dignified father would demand and how a loving father would freely forgive.

What would a father filled with dignity do? What would a father filled with dignity say? A dignified father would have lectured his son on how his actions had shamed him with embarrassment, not killed a calf for a feast to celebrate his coming home.

A dignified father would have thrown his son into guilt, not thrown him a party. A dignified father would not have interrupted his son's speech of self-imposed sanctions and penalties, seeking full payment for his pain. Then he would have read his son his prepared speech with all his demands for reinstatement with no thought of putting a robe on his back.

A dignified father would have given his son what he deserved, not given him shoes for his feet. A dignified father would have read him the riot act, not put a ring on his finger. And most of all, a dignified father would have never run to meet his son, because dignified men in Palestine did not run in public.

But the father sees his son first and runs to his son, lacking and losing all dignity. What a picture! The father, with no thought of his dignity, running to his son, who had no thought of the love and grace that was soon to embrace him.

They meet and the father hugs and kisses his son. As rehearsed, the son begins his prepared repentance speech "I have sinned…" But the son doesn't have a chance to finish his speech because his father interrupts him with plans for a "Welcome Home Feast." <u>Grace always interrupts our self-imposed sanctions and self-inflicted pain. Grace always trumps the confessions of a repentant heart of a life gone astray.</u>

Our son Rob is a man after God's own heart, except maybe when he is watching his Texas Aggies lose a football game. I'm convinced if Christ were to come again and choose twelve new disciples, Rob would be one of those chosen. He is one of those rare Christians who walks the straight and narrow day by day, year by year.

When he was about three years old, he had done something wrong and knew he needed to come to me to say he was sorry. It was winter and I was sitting in a chair by the fireplace watching him go back and forth from the kitchen to the hallway, praying he would come to me. I really wanted to say something, but I don't, sensing he needs to take the first step in seeking forgiveness. He has no idea of how much I want to forgive him, hold him, and love on him.

A log moves in the fireplace and I turn my head to see the fire, and when I turn my head back, I see Rob running to me as fast as his little legs would go, tears in his eyes and saying, "Daddy, I'm sorry, I'm sorry."

I open my arms as wide as they will go. He jumps in my lap and we embrace as I kiss his cheeks and forehead over and over, telling him how much I love him, with tears flowing down my cheeks.

I've never forgotten that night by the fireplace. His running, his tears, his words, his heart, our embrace, my tears, and God's word coming to life in our den by the fireplace.

After Rob climbed off my lap, I could think of nothing but the story Jesus told of the prodigal son and how much more the Lord is seeking our return from our times in the far country. And when He sees us take that first step back to Him in repentance, He will come running to embrace our brokenness. No lectures. No demands. No probationary periods. No dignity. Yes, there are always consequences to our actions in the far country, but given to Him in repentance can still bring Him Glory.

Have you ever been to the far country? Are you there now? Do you have concerns and doubts to His response of your return? Have you been preparing your "speech of repentance" to Him? Do you think you don't deserve a second chance, or a third, a fourth…?

Don't outthink His grace. Don't underestimate His love. Don't shortchange His forgiveness. Don't miss His first step to you after you take your first step to Him. Don't settle in a life with the pigs when you can embrace a life of love and forgiveness with the Father.

Aren't you thankful we serve a God who does not seek the dignity He could rightfully demand but the Glory He so wonderfully deserves? The cross was meant to inflict as much pain as possible while at the same time stripping one of all dignity. No, the cross at Calvary was not a place of dignity, but it was a place of Glory, the greatest Glory the world has ever known.

Could there be someone in your life, a brother or sister, a son or daughter, a mother or father, or a dear friend who is staying in the far country because they are more fearful of your justified dignity than believing and trusting in your love and loyalty? Is your dignity keeping His Glory in the far country? If God takes no thought of dignity, should we? Could it be that the Lord wants us to exchange our dignity for a new pair of jogging shoes?

His Glory. His binoculars.

His Glory, His Loaves

MATTHEW 14:21, 22 "THE NUMBER of those who ate was about five thousand men, besides women and children. Immediately, Jesus made his disciples get into the boat…"

MARK 6:42 "THEY ALL ATE and were satisfied, and the disciples picked up twelve baskets of broken pieces of bread and fish."

LUKE 9:11 "HE WELCOMED THEM and spoke to them about the kingdom of God and healed those who needed healing."

JOHN 6:9 "HERE IS A boy with five small barley loaves and two small fish, but how far will they go among so many."

JOHN 6:15 "JESUS, KNOWING THAT they intended to come and make Him king by force…"

What a picnic! We all know about this miracle, the only miracle mentioned in all four of the Gospels. Jesus takes the lunch given to Him by a little boy, a lunch consisting of five small loaves of bread and two tiny fish, and feeds five thousand men plus women and children, maybe fifteen thousand total.

All day long He taught about the kingdom of God, healed the sick, and then fed them until all were satisfied. Everything was going great until…. Let's push the pause button for a second and let our imaginations run for a moment.

Let's give the little boy who gave his sack lunch to Jesus a name, say Tommy. Now imagine Tommy as one little boy prone to exaggeration, telling stories of make-believe and sometimes getting into trouble for doing so. And then we can imagine Tommy's mother as one who often heard, "Do you want to know what your Tommy just did?"

It's late in the day and Tommy walks in the house after spending all day at the picnic. "Tommy, is that you?" his mom asks. "Yes, ma'am," he replies.

"What did you do today? Did you eat all the lunch I packed for you, all five loaves and the two fish?" "Mom, you're not going to believe what happened today! I gave my lunch to this man named Jesus and He took it and then fed thousands and thousands of people out of my little food basket. And after everyone ate, there were twelve baskets of food still left. It was unbelievable."

She replies, "You're right, it is unbelievable. I've told you before about the consequences of making up stories. Now go to your room."

"But, Mom," he answers with no response from her.

Now imagine Mom going to the market the next morning and someone asking her, "Are you Tommy's mother?"

She replies, "Yes, I am," and then waits, expecting to hear about some kind of trouble he had gotten into at the picnic.

"You must be so very proud of Tommy." "Excuse me?"

"The whole town is talking about what Jesus did with the lunch basket Tommy gave Him. Feeding all those thousands of people. Truly unbelievable."

Can't you just see Mom hurrying home, and when seeing Tommy, says, "Son, I'm so sorry I didn't believe you yesterday and sending you to your room. I'm truly sorry, and I'm also truly proud of you and what you did."

Do you think Mom ever thought the five loaves and two fish that she packed for Tommy's lunch that day would be part of the only miracle of Jesus mentioned in all four of the Gospels? Do you think when we are in heaven and someone introduces us to a smiling woman who says to us, "Welcome to eternity. I'm Tommy's mother," we will immediately know who she is? And we will see Tommy in the background, climbing on top of a harp, hoping Mom doesn't turn around to see.

Now back to the real story. All was going well, the teaching, the healings, and the feeding. But then things began to turn. John writes, "Jesus, knowing they intended to come and make Him king by force…" (John 6:15) And Matthew writes, "Immediately Jesus made the disciples get into the boat and go on ahead of Him to the other side, while He dismissed the crowd." (Matthew 14:22)

It appears the crowd and the disciples all got caught up in everything and began to think, "He can heal us when we are sick, teach us when we need instruction, and feed us when we are hungry. Let's make Him our king."

And at that, the picnic was over. He made the disciples get into the boat and then dismissed the crowd. (The word "made" in the Greek means "to compel," as a father disciplining his son.)

It's as if He was saying to the disciples, "You should have known better. I've told you over and over I'm seeking followers who desire My love, not just My loaves. My heart, not just My healings. My mercy, not just My miracles. My Glory, not just My gifts. Now get into the boat. Now!" Then Jesus went up into the hills all by Himself to pray.

And when the crowd that followed Him found Him on the other side of the lake, He told them, "I tell you the truth, you are looking for Me, not because you saw miraculous signs, but because you ate the loaves and had your fill." (John 6:25, 26)

Talk about a statement. A scripture that gets the spiritual scalpel out and starts dissecting what's in our heart for us to see what we are truly seeking. Are we looking for Him to fill our hands or to fill our hearts? To stockpile our pantry or to spread His Glory? Seeking what God can do for us or through us? Seeking Him or gifts from Him? Could it be that we bring God greater Glory when we seek to reflect the love in His heart rather than seeking the loaves in His hands? Greater Glory when we seek the "bread of life" and not "the bread of man?"

So many lessons to be learned from this miracle, so many things God can teach us. But know this, God can take insignificant me (you) with my (your) small little basket of five loaves and two fish, and when given to Him, can use it to feed others and bring Him Glory. And after He does so, when we look back, we will say like Tommy, "It was unbelievable." And all for His Glory.

His Glory. His picnic.

His Glory, His Question

JOHN 5:1-9 "SOME TIME LATER, Jesus went up to Jerusalem for a feast of the Jews. Now there is in Jerusalem near the Sheep Gate a pool, which in Aramaic is called Bethesda and which is surrounded by five covered colonnades. Here a great number of disabled people used to lie– the blind, the lame, the paralyzed. One who was there had been an invalid for thirty-eight years. When Jesus saw him lying there and learned that he had been in this condition for a long time, he asked him, 'Do you want to get well?'

'Sir,' the invalid replied, 'I have no one to help me into the pool when the water is stirred. While I am trying to get in, someone else goes down ahead of me.'

Then Jesus said to him, 'Get up! Pick up your mat and walk.' At once the man was cured; he picked up his mat and walked."

They lay there, the blind, the lame, the paralyzed. They lay there by the pool, not seeking a tan, but wanting to be the first in the pool after the water was stirred, a superstition that they believed would heal them. Imagine them all poolside with every eye fixed on the water. They lay there, wanting to be healed, wanting to walk, wanting to see, wanting to just move a limb. They lay there, wanting it to be their turn, their time, their healing.

Jesus walks by the pool and sees one of them lying on a mat, a man, an invalid, whose mat had been his home for thirty-eight years. Then He asks him, "Do you want to get well?" (It is my understanding that in the Greek text, the word "will" is used, not "want." He said, "Do you will to get well?")

Many were there by the pool. Did He heal others while He was poolside? If not, why not? Why him, why this man? Why did He ask him if he "willed" to get well? What did He see in him when He saw him lying there? Did He see this man through years and years of frustration and disappointment giving in to an acceptance of being carried and cared for? Did He see a man whose daily defeats had emptied his will, a man comfortable with his rationalizations and excuses? Did He see a man who needed his will to be stirred, not the water in the pool? Jesus, in love, in compassion, cut through his emotions and his feelings to this man's will, to the core of his being, where rationalizations, justifications, and excuses don't cut it, or stand up.

We laugh. We cry. We desire. We feel. All healthy and part of our created DNA. We smile at weddings and cry at funerals. We have tears of joy and tears of sorrow. We feel strong at times and weak at others.

We want to be better, live better. We want to volunteer more, give more, care more. We want to be more disciplined with our time and our talents. We want to pray more, to read more of God's word, to walk straighter.

But sometimes our desires of "wanting to" take us poolside because they remain a "want to" in our mind and not a "will to" deep within our heart and soul. And over time, like the man on the mat, we get comfortable with our own rationalizations and excuses, comfortable being poolside.

Have you ever been by that pool? Ever been blind? Blind to others? Their needs, their pain? Have you ever been lame? Have a hard time moving where God was leading? Difficult moving to others? Ever been paralyzed? Paralyzed by fear? By guilt? By anger? By hopelessness? By sorrow? By self pity? By confusion of mistaking "wanting to" for the "will to"?

Jesus told the man to "get up, pick up, and go." And the man was cured and got up, and picked up the mat and began to carry what had carried him for thirty-eight years. It doesn't matter how you got on the mat, whether by your own poor choices or by life unfairly throwing you down on it. God doesn't want you to stay there, to stay down.

I had just pitched a good game, only to lose 2 to 1. It was a day game in spring training in Florida and I couldn't wait to call my parents for some much-needed sympathy and verbal pats on the back.

Dad answered the phone that night and I immediately told him about my outstanding pitching performance resulting in a loss. He then asked with a tone in his voice that could have only come with ice water in his veins, "Is that about it?"

I'm thinking, "Isn't that enough?" and "Where is your compassion?" But I answer, "Yes, sir."

He then asked, "Any hospitals out there in Florida?"

Now I'm more confused than ever. What do hospitals have to do with my pitching performance? But again, I quickly respond, "Yes sir."

He asked again in that same cold penetrating voice, "Any nursing homes out there in Florida?"

I tell him, "Yes sir."

He asked again with an abrupt, short voice, "Any rehab centers out there in Florida?"

Now this is getting old, I tell myself. Of course there are rehab centers. Of course there are nursing homes. Of course there are hospitals. But I don't dare share my thoughts and feelings about his seemingly meaningless and pointless questions. I again simply say, "Yes sir."

His voice then changed to a more inquisitive nature and asked, "What time do you have to be at the ball park tomorrow?"

I quickly answer, "Three o'clock."

He then said, "Rob, why don't you get up early and visit some patients at all those places and give me a call tomorrow night."

Dad knew I was "on the mat" of self-pity. Dad knew the way "off the mat" was to feed, give, and help someone else. Dad not only knew the words that Jesus told Peter, "Feed My sheep," (John 21:17) he lived them!

Many years later when Dad was dying of cancer, Mom told me he probably sent over 1,000 letters in the last year of his life. Letters of "Happy Birthday." Letters of "Praying for you." Letters of "Congratulations." Letters of "Get Well Soon." Letters of "Encouragement." Letters of "Sympathy."

About two months before he died, I called him and mentioned that maybe he should save his strength by not getting up to write all those letters. Bad mistake. His response and tone of voice brought back unpleasant memories of a prior conversation many years earlier regarding hospitals, nursing homes, and rehab centers. He said firmly, "Rob, the day I stop thinking and doing for others and start thinking of myself is the day I will die."

Cancer may have thrown Dad's body "on the mat," but he refused through his will to let his mind, heart, and soul go there so he could continue to "feed His sheep." About a week before he died the letter writing stopped, but not the "feeding." Doctors, nurses, hospice personnel, friends, neighbors, recipients of his letters, and all who came by or called continued to be fed by a man of God, who in his living and in his dying reflected God's Glory like none other.

God created you. God knows you. He knows your DNA. He believes in you. And He is saying to you, "Get up, pick up, and go." You were created to bring God Glory, a Glory that is rarely reflected poolside. But when you do "get up, pick up, and go," your eyes will be opened to see the needs of others, your walk will take you to the straight and narrow, and whatever has paralyzed you will bound you no more, and all for His Glory. Do you want to or will to?

Jesus knew a lot about the will. He prayed it. He lived it. In Matthew 6:9, Jesus says, "This is how you should pray," and part of that prayer (we call it the Lord's Prayer) was "Your will be done." And three times in the garden of Gethsemane, as He was overwhelmed with sorrow, Jesus prayed, "Your will be done."

Aren't you thankful "God so loved the world" He sent His son to be born in a manger so that one day He could help us off the mat?

Aren't you thankful Jesus prayed for His Father's will? Aren't you thankful Jesus willed His way to the cross?

Aren't you thankful His prayer of "Thy will be done" was answered on the cross?

Aren't you thankful the submitted will of Jesus to the purposed will of God together brought God Glory and us eternal life?

His Glory. His will.

His Glory, His Wedding

JOHN 2:3 "WHEN THE WINE was gone, Jesus' mother said to Him, 'They have no more wine.'"

JOHN 2:4 "JESUS REPLIED, 'MY time has not yet come.'"

JOHN 2:6, 7 "NEARBY STOOD six stone water jars, the kind used by the Jews for ceremonial washing, each holding from twenty to thirty gallons. Jesus said to the servants, 'Fill the jars with water'; so they filled them to the brim."

JOHN 2:11 "THIS, THE FIRST of His miraculous signs, Jesus performed in Cana of Galilee. He thus revealed His Glory, and His disciples put their faith in Him."

JOSHUA 1:5 "…I WILL NEVER leave you or forsake you."

MATTHEW 28:20 "…AND SURELY I will be with you always."

You know the story. Jesus, His disciples, and His mother have been invited to a wedding in Cana in Galilee, the bride's hometown. The wine runs out, a terrible embarrassment for the bride, groom, and their parents. His mother informs Him of the problem, to which He replies, "My time has not yet come," but then proceeds to turn six stone jars full to the brim with water into choice wine. Embarrassment diverted. Glory revealed.

Why His first miracle of turning water into wine at a small, intimate wedding? Why not feed 5,000 men, plus women and children, with five loaves and two fish as His first miracle? Wouldn't the feeding of the masses bring more Glory, more attention, more splash, and more headlines in the *Jerusalem Chronicle* or *Galilee Post*?

Why was His "time not yet come," and then it came? What changed? Why first reveal His Glory at a wedding? Why this wedding?

Our daughter, Callie, and her husband, Tony, gave me the great honor and privilege of speaking at their wedding several years ago. From the moment they asked I was excited, and looked forward to having a small part on their big day.

The day of the wedding arrived. My brother Reg (the kindest, most thoughtful man of God I know, and a brilliant doctor) had flown in from Missouri with all his love, kindness, and gifts. (No one can out give Reg, no one.) I'm excited. I rehearse my speech one last time and then I'm off to the church, full of joy, smiling all the way.

But as soon as I enter the church, my smiling face becomes a floodgate of tears. I cry and cry and cannot stop. I make my way to a restroom, seeking to be alone while trying to pull myself together. I do so after a few minutes, and then proceed to the sanctuary for wedding pictures. After the last photo is taken, I sense another round of tears, so I quickly return to my secluded restroom with tears, with questions, and with a prayer. "Lord, you know I've got to speak in a few minutes and I don't want to embarrass Callie and Tony, so please help me."

The stream of tears has slowed to a small trickle, and with the wedding only fifteen minutes away, I leave my crying chamber in search of Callie. I see her in the near distance and she is radiant in all her beauty. I walk to her and tell her, "You look gorgeous, absolutely gorgeous. More than ever."

She smiles and so politely says, "Thanks, Daddy." I asked her if she would like to pray together and she says, "I would love to. I really need it." I take her hand, we bow our heads. I start praying, and then back come the tears that render me speechless.

Callie, sensing the situation with all her love and tenderness, says, "Daddy, it's okay if you can't speak at the wedding. I understand. I love you, Daddy."

As she reaches out to hug me, I'm thinking, "Here I am, the father of the bride, the one supposed to be giving her confidence, composure, assurance, and strength. Yet here she is, giving it to me. Definitely not how I planned this, not at all."

I don't have much time to dwell on her strength and my lack of it because the organist starts to play the wedding march, the guests all stand, and down the aisle we go. A beautiful, radiant bride, my little girl, full of joy with head held high for all to see, and the father of the bride in tears, with head down, seeking to avoid eye contact so no one could see. Quite the pair.

The aisle going down isn't that long, but long enough for my mind to become a "pinball of thoughts," bouncing all over the place. Still in tears, I think back to my time in athletics seeking to convince myself of the toughness I once had. "Remember, you played football in high school with several concussions, broken fingers, and numerous sprains, cuts, and bruises. And you didn't cry then. Remember when you were fourteen, and you kept pitching in a game with a sore elbow until you broke it throwing a fastball? Your arm just dangled in pain, but you didn't cry then. You can do this. Remember the knee surgery and open-heart surgery and the pain with both? You didn't cry then. You can do this."

I start to look up with some renewed confidence until that "pinball of thoughts" bounces off in another direction. Maybe this isn't about toughness at all. Maybe God just doesn't want you to speak. Remember all those horrible things you said to Him several years ago in your anger. Maybe He doesn't want you speaking at His church. Maybe you crossed the line in what you said, what you thought, and what you believed. Maybe He said "enough" and left you and is no longer in you. After all, you've spoken many times before and this has never happened.

I lower my head back down in doubt. We're almost to the front of the church and then that pinball bounces to one last thought which makes me think, "Game over." How am I going to tell all these people I can't talk if I can't talk? How am I going to apologize if I can't talk? How am I going to tell the preacher I can't talk if I can't talk? I offer one last prayer, "Lord, if you are still in me and can hear me, please help me. Please, I don't want to embarrass Callie or Tony, they deserve the best."

We arrive at the front of the church with Rev. Tim Owens (a truly special man of God with a heart for God) there to greet us with a smile, and then with words of welcome to all the guests. As rehearsed, when Tim finishes talking, he and I walk up four steps, take four steps back, turn around together, he moves off to the side, and then I begin my speech. Each step up and each step back I'm still thinking, "How am I going to tell everyone I can't talk if I can't talk?" I turn around. It's "go time" with no place to go and with absolutely no idea of what is going to happen. None. I'm empty. I'm speechless. I'm afraid.

And then, facing all the guests, the tears quit flowing and I hear a soft tender voice in my heart say, "I love you. You're Mine forever and always will be. I have never and will never leave you nor forsake you. And now I will speak through you."

The words start flowing just as I had rehearsed so many times in the privacy of my home. Prayer answered. Embarrassment diverted. Another miracle at a wedding. Only the Lord, Callie, and I will ever know what truly happened. Think again.

The next day I'm in our living room having a conversation with my brother, Reg, before he and his family leave for the airport. We're laughing, having a great time, and then he asked me, "Do you have a speaking voice?"

"What do you mean?" I asked.

He repeated the question. "Do you have a speaking voice, one you use when you speak to a crowd?" And before I can digest the question, he says, "Rob, I'm your brother. I know you and I know your voice. I've heard it for about fifty years and that wasn't your voice I heard at the wedding."

I am taken aback with his question. His insight takes me to the Lord. It was as if God was saying to me through Reg, "Don't take what happened at the wedding lightly. Don't pass off your crying and tears as just emotion and nerves. I emptied you at the wedding, filled your eyes with tears, and rendered you speechless for the purpose of revealing Myself to you and speaking through you. You were emptied, just like the six stone jars in Cana. You were filled with My Spirit, just as the water jars were filled with water. You were both filled to the brim, so you, and no one else, could add to or take away what I and I alone had done.

"And just as I turned the water into choice wine at that wedding in Cana, I turned many things at that wedding of your daughter and My child, Callie. I turned your doubts of My presence in you, of My life in you, into an assurance which should never again be questioned. I turned your questions of 'Did I sin too much and go too far' into a resounding no. I turned you to the scriptures, to My word, and to My promise of which you were so familiar. 'For I am convinced…nor anything else in all creation, will be able to separate us from the love of God that is in Christ Jesus our Lord.' (Romans 8:38) I took that scripture you had memorized in your mind and engraved it in your heart. I turned off the flow of tears so I could speak through you. And forever remember that it was I, the Lord God, that turned your day of confusion and of doubt at Callie's and Tony's wedding into My day of Glory."

Sometimes God empties us so He can then fill us. He may empty us in different ways and for different reasons. The emptying is rarely one of pleasure, but one of purpose. He may see the need to empty us of some of our doubts, or some misguided beliefs, or some confidence in our flesh, or maybe something of value that we continue to claim as ours.

He empties us not to punish us, but to redeem us, and a redeemed us brings Him Glory.

His Glory. His emptying. His filling.

His Glory, His Aroma

MATTHEW 5:39 "IF SOMEONE STRIKES you on the right cheek, turn to him the other also."

JOHN 12:3 "THEN MARY TOOK a pint of pure nard, an expensive perfume; she poured it on Jesus' feet and wiped His feet with her hair. And the house was filled with the fragrance of the perfume."

While the disciples may have been continuing their discussion amongst them of who was the greatest and who deserved to be seated on His right and left, Mary was quietly kneeling at His feet in true humility, in true expression, and in true love.

The cross was only about a week away and one must wonder if she saw something in His eyes or maybe heard something in His voice. Or did His presence bring out the very essence of her being, one that took her to His feet, one that took her hair down (it was not dignified for a woman to let her hair down in public), one that took a year's wage of perfume to pour on His feet, and one that took her hair to wipe the perfume on His feet. Mary, pouring out her heart as she poured the perfume on His feet. Mary, taking no thought of personal dignity or pride, just taking Him and loving Him as she knelt at His feet.

Has your pride ever kept you from loving our Lord? Has your dignity ever prevented you from kneeling at His feet and serving Him in true humility? Have your priorities ever kept the lid on the perfume bottle, preventing the aroma of God from filling the room where you live or work?

Pat and Desi Marek are special people, special Christians, with a special love for each other, for others, and for our Lord. We grew up in the same town (College Station, Texas), went to the same high school (A&M Consolidated), and lived in the same neighborhood. Pat and I played on the same football and baseball teams, and later in life we coached our kids in Little League. We were friends.

And then something happened during those Little League years that kept us from speaking to one another for almost seven years. Pat only thought he was right, but I knew I was right, because my pride and dignity kept telling me so, again and again. During this time, I developed a case of spiritual lockjaw, a jaw so locked into pride, ego, and self-righteousness that it prevented me from turning my cheek.

Then one morning I woke up in a hospital room after needing five bypasses through open-heart surgery. The room was already full of flowers but my wife Susan had strategically placed some new flowers on the left side of my bed.

I asked her, "Who are those flowers from?"

Knowing the history and knowing whom they were from, she says, "Look and see." I turned my head to see a beautiful bouquet of flowers that had been sent by those who had, in Christ-like love, turned their cheeks, those being Pat and Desi Marek.

After shedding a few tears, my senses opened up, and then I realized their flowers had a distinct smell from all the others. A certain fragrance of forgiveness and love that only a surrendered heart with emptied pride and turned cheeks can bring into a room, the sweet aroma of two lives who had knelt at the feet of Jesus, bringing Glory to God.

Pat had just recently gone to Houston to receive a "new heart" through heart transplant surgery. A "new heart" with the same spirit of a loving God pumping life into him and to those fortunate others that cross his path. As for me, I will always remember the "old heart," the one God used to show me how turning the other cheek and kneeling at the feet of Jesus with true humility can bring so much aroma into a room, into a life, while bringing God so much Glory.

Do you have a cheek that needs to be turned? An extra mile you need to walk? A particular pride you need to swallow? A certain person you need to add to your prayer list? Yes, that one who has really hurt you. A knee that needs to be bent in prayer? A Bible you need to pick up?

Is the Lord wanting you to be a Pat and Desi Marek in someone's life? Does He desire from you to be that "sweet aroma of God" in a relationship gone sour? Someone once said, "The impact we have on others depends on the impact the Holy Spirit has on us." That impact brings sweet aroma into a room, into a relationship, into a testimony, into a life, and all for the Glory of God.

His Glory. His sweet aroma.

His Glory, His Triumph

JOHN 19:30 "IT IS FINISHED."

"It is finished." The last words of Jesus spoken on the cross. Words spoken with a sigh of relief from one beaten and broken in defeat? Not hardly. The scriptures are clear. His last words were said in a shout of victory. (The same words that would have been spoken by a football team in Jerusalem going undefeated and winning the state championship game.) He had completed the work His Father had given Him to do. Mission accomplished. Purpose fulfilled. Eternity now made possible to all who believe. All things said and done for the Glory of God. "It is finished," not "I am finished."

But before He said, "It is finished," He said, "Father, forgive them, for they do not know what they are doing." (Luke 23:34) Forgiving those throwing insults into His face. Forgiving those nailing spikes into His flesh. Forgiving them. Forgiving you. Forgiving me. Had the words

"Father forgive them" ever been spoken before by anyone, anywhere, on any cross? Was this the first time anyone ever heard these words at Calvary?

Is there a place in your life where you need to say, "I forgive you," for the first time? A place in your marriage? A place at work? At school? A place with your parents. Your kids? The place is not so much a lesson in geography as it is a place in the heart that has not yet been yielded to the Lord. Is there someone in your life who needs to hear those words for the first time?

Could Jesus have said, "It is finished," without first saying, "Father, forgive them?" Was His final act of reflecting the Glory of God to completion to forgive those at the cross?

In Acts 7, Stephen speaks to the Sanhedrin and finishes his speech with a few choice words that incite them into stoning him to death. While they were stoning him, his final words were, "Lord, do not hold this sin against them." (Acts 7:60) But right before he had said those words of forgiveness, he had prayed, "Lord Jesus, receive my spirit." (Acts 7:59) Could Stephen have forgiven those with stones in their hands without first giving the Lord his spirit? Could Stephen have forgiven them without being "full of the Holy Spirit?" (Acts 7:55)

"When Stephen, full of the Holy Spirit, looked up to heaven he saw the Glory of God…" (Acts 7:55) Did God, knowing Stephen's heart and seeing his courage and conviction, reveal His Glory knowing Stephen was going to reveal His Spirit of forgiveness to those with stones in their hands, those same hands that once held spikes at Calvary?

Is God waiting to reveal His Glory to us, knowing we are soon going to reveal His Spirit of forgiveness to someone with stones in their hands? Stones of abuse? Stones of anger? Of hate? Stones of jealousy? Of gossip? Is His Glory waiting?

Stephen also saw "Jesus <u>standing</u> at the right hand of God." (Acts 7:55) This is the only time in the New Testament when Jesus is <u>standing</u>

by God and not sitting. Jesus, <u>standing</u> to receive this man's courage, this man's loyalty, this man's love, this man's forgiveness, this man's heart, this man's spirit.

I looked up and saw Mrs. Sharon Oman <u>standing</u> with "the note" in her hand. A few minutes before, "the note" was in my hand as I sat at my desk in her world geography class. She was "the teacher," a very, very pretty teacher. I was "the student," a junior in high school and a very, very dumb student. "The note" was from "the girlfriend," a very, very angry one, and rightfully so.

My girlfriend had heard enough of my talk of the many compliments I was giving my teacher regarding her beauty. And now it was her turn to talk, and talk she did through "the note," given to me right before I walked into Mrs. Oman's class. I knew I shouldn't have opened "the note" in class because the consequences could be painful. If a teacher caught a student reading something other than class-related material, he or she could send you to the principal, read the material to the class, or both. But I was smarter than "the teacher" because I put "the note" on the pages of my opened geography book, hidden from her view in front of the room. I thought I was clever, really clever.

So I sat there reading "the note," oblivious to everything and anyone around me. "The note" was full of derogatory comments about my beautiful geography teacher and me. She held nothing back, letting both of us have it in full fury. I was almost finished reading "the note" when a hand reached down from behind me and took "the note."

I had become so absorbed reading "the note," that I failed to look up and see that she had vacated her chair in front of the room and walked quietly behind me. She took "the note" with her to her chair behind her desk. I quickly followed without permission to do so and begged her to not read "the note." I volunteered for all kinds of punishment if she just wouldn't read "the note." Nothing worked.

She quietly reminded me of the choices she held regarding the consequences of my actions, and asked me to go back to my desk and sit down. I did so, only to look up and see her reading "the note," page by page. With each page, my head lowered in extreme embarrassment and shame. I knew it was all my fault. I knew I had caused my girlfriend's jealousy. I knew I was wrong to read "the note" in class. I knew the consequences of my actions, and knew that at any moment my teacher would start reading "the note" to the class. I could just hear her saying, "Class, before we begin our geography lesson for today, I would like to read a note that Rob thought was so important he chose to open and read it at his desk a few minutes ago."

I looked up and saw her <u>standing</u> with "the note" in her hand as she then said, "Class, would you please open your books to page 146 and…" I looked up in disbelief to see she was <u>standing</u> in front of my row looking at me with a soft smile on her face. <u>Standing</u> with compassion. <u>Standing</u> with sensitivity. <u>Standing</u> with understanding. <u>Standing</u> with forgiveness. <u>Standing</u> before me. <u>Standing</u> for me.

The bell rang thirty minutes later, and as I walked out of her class, Mrs. Oman stopped me, smiled, and handed me back "the note". Not a word was said, but her silence would forever stay in my heart. As I walked down the hall to my next class, I looked at "the note" to find that she had written in red ink the words, "Love is grand, no?"

"The note" was full of stones thrown in her direction. Stones of anger. Stones of jealousy. Stones thrown of which I was to blame. But she said nothing, only smiled. <u>Her smile spoke of a heart yielded to Him. Her silence spoke of a spirit given to Him.</u>

Is this the kind of silence that Jesus wants to hear? Is this the kind of forgiveness that Jesus seeks? Is this the kind of spirit to which Jesus <u>stands</u>?

Will Jesus <u>stand</u> up to receive your spirit? My spirit? Will He <u>stand</u> up to receive us into heaven? Have our lives reflected the Lord's Spirit with such courage, compassion, and forgiveness that He would <u>stand</u> up to receive us into eternity? Could it be that He will only <u>stand</u> up if we <u>stand</u> up through a life of reflecting His Glory by <u>standing</u> up for Him?

His Glory. His standing.

His Glory, His Treasures and Rewards

Matthew 6:20 "But lay up for yourselves treasures in heaven…"

Matthew 6:4, 6, 18 "Then your Father, who sees what is done in secret, will reward you."

John 6:25 "When they found Him…"

John 6:26 "Jesus answered, 'I tell you the truth. You are looking for me, not because you saw miraculous signs, but because you ate the loaves and had your fill.'"

They sought Him. They found Him. They wanted more, maybe even expecting more. In the miracle where Jesus feeds the multitudes with five loaves and two fish, everyone obeys. The disciples obey Jesus and the multitudes obey the disciples. They obeyed. They ate. They had their fill. Jesus departs. They seek Him. They find Him. But why? Did they want more? Did they expect more?

The story is told of a wealthy Texas rancher who owned thousands of acres of land. One day he decides to check on a piece of his land that he had not been to in several years, a barren tract far away from the ranch house. Once there, he finds three huge barns, one of which is twice the size of the other two.

Confused and curious, he enters one of the barns and is quickly greeted by a worker who says, "Welcome to satan's barns. Let me give you a tour." The rancher nods his head with much uncertainty.

The tour begins. The worker says, "As you can see, on both sides of the aisle are stalls, each one containing thousands upon thousands of seeds, and each stall is labeled and identified. This stall contains seeds of greed, and that one is full of seeds of lust. Next we have seeds of envy, seeds of jealousy, seeds of hate, seeds of bitterness, seeds of selfishness, and seeds of pride. Those "pride seeds," by the way, are really special, and we are always in short supply because they work so well."

They enter the next barn after the rancher had seen many more seeds waiting to be planted into the hearts of men and women. The helper continues, "Now this barn is full of seeds of a different kind, but they still work well. This first stall is full of seeds of hopelessness. Next to them, seeds of thanklessness, seeds of despair, seeds of giving up, seeds of purposelessness, seeds of darkness, seeds of gloom, and one of my favorites, seeds of praiselessness. There are plenty more of these kinds of seeds, but I can't wait to show you our prized seed. As you can see, this barn is twice the size of the other two, yet it contains only one seed."

"One seed?" the rancher asks.

"Just one, but it is a very, very special seed. We have found that when this seed takes root, all the other seeds begin to grow as well. The other seeds feed off this one special seed. And I've saved the best for last. This seed works best in the most committed of Christians and has brought down many a believer."

"So tell me, what one seed could do so much devastation to a committed Christian?" the rancher anxiously asks.

The helper says with pride, "These are the seeds of obligation, the greatest of all seeds. Once this seed takes root, the believer becomes convinced that each act of goodness, faithfulness, kindness, and obedience is a deposit into his "spiritual account" with God, thus giving him the right to present Him with a blank check with the words, "I've been good to You and for You, now I've come to collect." In other words, they come to believe God owes them. God is obligated to them. It's like they believe when they have finished the "Seven Step Program of Obedience," all sevens will turn up on God's jackpot of blessings, thus pouring out all kinds of earthly delights and treasures into their lives. So when problems arise, the business goes under, the wife leaves, the child dies, the husband cheats, the financial problems mount, or their health falters, they go out the back door of the church, walk away from God, and rarely come back. That is why they are our most cherished seed."

Why do we seek the Lord? Why do we obey Him? In Matthew 7, we are told to ask, seek, and knock. In Matthew 6, Jesus says there are rewards for giving, praying, and fasting in secret. Do we seek Him to Glorify Him? Do we obey Him to Glorify Him? Do we ask, seek, and knock to bring Him Glory? Do we give and fast to bring Him Glory? Do our prayers seek to Glorify Him? Could it be that our greatest obedience to God might bring forth our deepest disappointment from God while at the same time bringing Glory for God?

Could it be that God rewards our giving, our obedience, with blessings that might bring us pain and suffering but bring Him adoration and Glory? Can the treasures we lay up in heaven come from tears laid down by our obedience on earth?

Through Matthew, God tells us that we will receive rewards and blessings for our humble and quiet obedience to His word. Can these rewards and blessings come from the very heart of God, shaped by the hand of God for the Glory of God? Can they be shaped in an array of sizes coming from all directions? Some bringing tears of sadness, others bringing tears of joy, both for His Glory? Can we see His hand, His fingerprints, on those circumstances and situations where our obedience in seeking to bring God Glory brings us to our knees?

We can lay hold of His promise of blessings and rewards. When they come is up to Him. Where they come is up to Him. How they come is up to Him. So whether they come here on earth or later in heaven, or both, they come from His hands, His heart, for His Glory, and all without obligation.

His Glory. His blessings.

His Glory, His GPS

As mentioned in another chapter, my Dad was a genius with an engineering degree from Texas A&M. I can only imagine how he felt when he realized his oldest son (that would be me) did not share any of his "intelligence genes." That realization may have come when I was younger, but for sure in eighth grade.

One night he was helping me with my algebra homework, having put the problem and the fifteen steps to solve it on a huge blackboard in our home. He started with Step 1, A=B. He then said, "Now in Step 2…"

I interrupted him and asked, "Why doesn't a=a and b=b?" So for the next fifteen minutes he tried to explain to me why a=b. It didn't work. "That still makes no sense," I replied with a confused look on my face. So for the next thirty minutes he tried to explain it another way. That didn't work either, so he erased the board and any thought of his oldest son ever becoming an engineer.

Fast forward to when I'm about forty. He called me and asked for directions to a place my family and I had recently visited. I said, "Dad, it's easy to find. Take the first exit past the Exxon station, then when you come to the light, take a right and it's not too far from there."

Well, as you can imagine, this engineer on the other phone had a built in GPS system that only registered specific names and numbers, all requiring directions in north, south, east, or west. No rights. No lefts. He asked nicely, "What is the name of the exit?"

I replied, "I don't know, just the first one past the Exxon station."

He said, "No exit name, no exit number?"

I now sense some frustration, so I carefully answered, "Dad, I'm sure the exit has a name and a number, but I don't know what they are. Just past the Exxon station."

Then he asked, "Is right east or west?"

Again I have no answer. "I don't know, just go right at the light." At that, I can now see his internal GPS going haywire as evidenced by all the smoke coming through the phone. And I'm sure he was then thinking, "If he (that would be me) never figured out how a could equal b, then how could he possibly know if right was east or west."

Our GPS systems were not compatible. His, the advanced high tech, 3D, HD supermodel. Mine, the beginner's model with training wheels included. His, longitude and latitude. Mine, up and down. His, east, west, north, and south. Mine, right and left. His, street names, numbers, and addresses. Mine, landmarks or sayings: "second left," "just past Grace Bible Church," or "if you see Chick-fil-A, you've gone too far."

In reading the Bible, especially Matthew, Mark, Luke, and John, it is clear Jesus had His own internal GPS. A GPS not only with directions, but directions with time. Directions of both where to go and where not to go. Directions of when to go and when not to go. His GPS was synchronized with the will of God with all directions pointing to the Glory of God.

The scriptures are filled with Jesus coming and going, staying and leaving, a GPS fine-tuned by prayer, much prayer.

1. John 4:4 "**Now He had to go through** Samaria."
2. John 4:40 "…and **He stayed two days**."
3. John 4:43 "**After the two days** He left for Galilee."
4. John 6:1 "**Sometime after this, Jesus crossed** to the far shore of the Sea of Galilee."
5. John 7:1 "After this, Jesus went around in Galilee, purposely **staying away** from Judea…"
6. John 7:9 "Having said this, He **stayed** in Galilee."
7. John 8:20 "Yet no one seized Him because **His time had not yet come**."
8. John 8:59 "At this, they picked up stones to stone Him, **but Jesus hid himself, slipping away** from the temple grounds."
9. John 10:39 "Again they tried to seize Him, **but He escaped their grasp**."
10. Luke 4:30 "But **He walked right through the crowd and went on His way**."

These are but a few of the scriptures regarding His GPS. For two and a half years His GPS took Him to people who needed healing, to places where He would teach, and to a tomb to resurrect a friend. And it also took Him away from those trying to seize Him and kill Him.

Why hide Himself? Why slip away? Why escape their grasp? Why did no one seize Him? Did anyone ever call Him names for hiding and walking away? Did anyone ever accuse Him of being a coward for hiding?

Or did He show great courage in walking away, knowing His time was not yet come? Did He show great restraint in avoiding confrontation because His GPS was telling Him, "Not now, not yet." **Did Jesus, Son** of Man, Son of God, hide Himself so as to not hinder the purposed timing of the will of God?

Then His GPS directed Him to Caesarea Philippi, a city with a history of worship to gods of baal, pan, and tiberius caesar. It was here, with the backdrop of all these earthly gods within sight, that Jesus asked His disciples, "But what about you? Who do you say I am?" (Matthew 16:15) And when Peter answered, **"You are the Christ," His GPS at that very moment pointed to Jerusalem, more specifically to a hill called Calvary.**

Now look at the scriptures revealing His GPS with new coordinates directing Him to **His Cross** and **His Glory**.

1. Luke 9:51 "As the time approached for Him to be taken up to heaven, **Jesus resolutely set out for Jerusalem.**"
2. Luke 13:22 "Then Jesus went through the towns and villages, **teaching as He made His way to Jerusalem.**"
3. Luke 17:11 **"Now, on His way to Jerusalem…"**
4. Luke 19:28 "After Jesus had said this, **He went on ahead, going up to Jerusalem.**"
5. John 13:1 **"Jesus knew that the time had come for Him to leave this world and go to the Father."**
6. John 17:1 **"Father, the time has come. Glorify Your Son."**
7. John 17:13 **"I am coming to you now."**
8. Mark 10:32 "They were on their way up to Jerusalem **with Jesus leading the way…**"

It would be a six-month journey from Caesarea Philippi to Jerusalem, with Jesus leading the way. He will hide no more. He will walk away no more. He will stay away no more. He will slip away no more. His time has now come. His hour is now approaching. He will lead the way. His disciples will have to quicken the pace to keep up. His GPS is set. His mind is set. His heart is set. His cross is set. Every step now will be one step closer to His cross, to **His Glory.**

Try and stop Him now and see what happens. Try and change His GPS set for Jerusalem and see what He says. Peter tried to when he told Jesus, "Never, Lord! This will never happen to you!" (Matthew 16:22)

And look at the response of Jesus. "Out of my sight, satan!" (Matthew 16:23) Jesus didn't say, "I appreciate that Peter is trying to protect me, but…" Nor did He say, "Maybe you're right, Peter. Let me rethink all of this." No, He called him satan.

Do you think when Peter was alone with the other disciples without Jesus that he said to them, "Can you believe it. He called me satan. He actually called me satan. You all heard Him, and I don't recall any of you trying to defend me. Fellows, something is going on. I've never seen Him like this before. I've never seen "that look" in His eyes before. Have you?"

No, no one had ever seen "that look" before because no one had ever seen Him with His GPS so fixed on Jerusalem before. "That look," which no one had ever seen before or will again because only He would take "that look" to the cross to save mankind from sin, and to then be called "that Savior."

What about you? Where does your internal GPS direct you? Do you set it or is it set every morning by prayer? Does your GPS seek a path to bring the Lord His greatest Glory? If God set your GPS to your "own Jerusalem," would you go? Are you dependent on your GPS, or can you go days, weeks, months, or years without it, seeking your own path?

Jesus said in John 16:28, "I came from the Father and entered the world; now I am leaving the world and **going back to the Father**." And in John 17:4 He said, "I have brought you Glory on earth by completing the work you gave me to do." His work was done. His work completed. His GPS had served to bring God Glory every day and by every step as He was directed. And when He said on the cross, "It is finished," there was no longer any need for His GPS to give Him directions, for He was going back home to be with His Father. He had been there before and knew His way back. He may not have needed His GPS to get back home, but He knew we did.

When we received Jesus into our heart to be our Lord and Savior, we also received His GPS with these directions, "Therefore go and make disciples of all nations, baptizing them in the name of the Father and of the Son and of the Holy Spirit, and teaching them to obey everything I have commanded you. And surely I will be with you always, to the very end of the age." (Matthew 28:19, 20)

Each one of us has received a GPS uniquely created by God for the sole purpose of bringing Glory to God. His directions are personal, knowing our gifts and talents. His directions come with power through our obedience, through prayer. Our GPS, given to us by God, may take us to those lost and without a GPS. May take us to that one person needing our help, our touch, our love. May take us to "our Jerusalem". But always, always our GPS will take us home to Him for His Glory.

His Glory. His GPS. Our GPS.

His Glory, His Upper Room

LUKE 22:12 "HE WILL SHOW you a large upper room…"

LUKE 22:15 "I HAVE EAGERLY desired to eat this Passover with you before I suffer."

LUKE 22:19 "…THIS IS MY body given for you, do this in remembrance of Me."

LUKE 22:20 "…THIS CUP IS the new covenant in My blood, which is poured out for you."

LUKE 22:31 "SIMON, SIMON, SATAN has asked to sift you as wheat. But I have prayed for you, Simon, that your faith may not fail. And when you have turned back, strengthen your brothers."

Judas has already agreed to betray Jesus. The deal has been cut. The money is now in his account at the Jerusalem National Bank. The planning is in the final stages. The blood is in the water. The sharks are circling in a frenzy. The time is near.

At the very same time, Jesus is preparing a Passover meal in an **upper room**, His final meal with the disciples before the cross. He will talk about blood, His blood, which will be poured out for them, for you, for me. He knows the blood in the water causing the frenzy will be His blood. He will share His heart with them, His final words before His death. The time is near. He knows it.

Imagine your time is near. Maybe it is. You know it. One week, one month, maybe two. What would you say to your family? Your spouse? Your kids? Your grandkids? Your parents? Your friends? As you are having one last meal together as a family, can you imagine what would be going through your mind with so much on your heart? What would you say knowing last words can be lasting words?

In the upper room, Jesus shares His heart with the disciples, His body broken for them, His blood poured out for them. Then He gets personal with Simon, real personal.

In the upper room, Jesus tells Simon (Peter) He has had a discussion with satan and that he is now a target of satan. Can you imagine how he must have felt? A target of satan, what could that mean?

Why me? Why the bull's-eye on my back? **Do you think Jesus and satan have ever discussed you? Is your life of such character and of such potential that satan has made you a target and has asked Jesus to sift you as wheat?**

In the upper room, Jesus tells Simon He is praying for him, a prayer that his faith would not fail, **not** that he would not fail. **Now can you imagine what Simon is thinking? He has gone from being a target on satan's list to a name on Jesus' prayer list.** Jesus is praying for Simon, for you. How does that stir your heart? But if you, as a child of God, pray for your children, how much more does He pray for us, His children?

In the upper room, Jesus tells Simon he will fail. He knows the three denials are right around the corner and the cock is clearing his throat. He also knows Judas will soon deny Him, betray Him, and fail Him.

Simon will fail, and then follow.

Judas will fail, and then flee.

Simon will fail, and then find repentance.

Judas will fail, and then find a rope.

Simon will cave in, and then come back.

Judas will cash in, and then check out.

Two men. Both failed. One turned his failing into a fatality. One turned his failing into a faithful follower. Our failings need not be final. Our failings need not make us a failure. And for sure, our failings need not be fatal.

In the upper room, Jesus tells Simon he will come back, and when he does, he will strengthen the others. Maybe Jesus knew the only thing that would silence the continued "sound of the cock crowing" in Simon's mind would be His final words to him, "And when you have turned back, strengthen your brothers." The world wants us to hear the "cock crow," always reminding us of our defeats. Our failures. Our denials. And that is why we must have an **upper room.**

My Dad's study was located upstairs in their home, his "**upper room.**" The room was filled with shelves and shelves of Bible study books. Books on the Old Testament. Books on the New Testament. Books in the Greek language. All kind of books.

But more importantly, his "upper room" was where he spent time in prayer, alone with God. A time when he spoke to God, and a time when God spoke to him through the scriptures. A time when God revealed to him he was to be a "living Bible," a walking example of the written word of God, a living life Glorifying Him.

Before his funeral, I walked upstairs to his "upper room". I wanted to be alone, to reflect, to cry. His bookshelves were full, displaying the heart of a man seeking to know God more and more. I walked into a closet and opened several boxes stacked in a corner almost hidden from view. Each box contained hundreds of "letters of appreciation", "certificates of service", "plaques of past presidencies," and countless "humanitarian awards".

Later, I found a local newspaper with his picture and obituary. His obituary could have been two or three pages full of his accomplishments, but he had told Mom to limit it to a few paragraphs. But there was one thing in his obituary that caught my full attention, something I had never known. The mayor of Wichita Falls, Texas, had proclaimed a "Bob Schleider Day" a few years earlier. I knew about the "Bob Schleider Day" in College Station, Texas, because all of our family was there at that reception, but I knew nothing of "the day" in Wichita Falls. I quickly asked my brothers, Rick and Reg, if they knew about the "Bob Schleider Day" in Wichita Falls. They both said no. I then asked Mom, and her reply was, "You know your Dad and how he believed in serving, just like in College Station."

I said, "Mom, I know all that, but why didn't he tell us, his own sons, about this special day. Only one in a million have one city designate a day in their honor, but he had two cities honor him, maybe one in a hundred million."

Her response was quick and heartfelt. "Rob, one of your Dad's favorite verses in the Bible was '... do not let the left hand know what your right hand is doing, so that your giving may be in secret.' (Matthew 6:3, 4) He did everything to Glorify the Lord, never seeking the praise of man, or his children."

Suddenly, his "upper room" became my "upper room", a place where God was speaking to me through the numerous awards stuffed in the back of a closet, through a condensed obituary, through a special day honoring him gone unknown to his children, and through the scriptures coming alive with the words of Jesus, "...do not let the left hand know what your right hand is doing, so that your giving may be in secret." (Matthew 6:3, 4) Looking back, the greatest gift this loving father gave me was the time he spent in his "upper room". Will my children say that about me one day? Will your children say that about you one day?

Do you have an **upper room**? A place where the Lord reveals to you not only who He is, but who you are as well? A place of continual remembrance of His body broken for you, and His blood shed for you? A place where He assures you of His belief and faith in you? A place where He calls you by name and then calls you to strengthen those around you? A place where He silences all sounds of the cock crowing? A place where the world has no say, no voice? A place where He can get real personal with you, like He did with Simon? A place where He shares His heart with you? A place where past, present, and future defeats, denials, and disappointments are turned into **Glory** for the Lord? A place where the God of all creation reminds you He created you to reflect His **Glory**? An **upper room,** your **upper room,** a place where Christ crucified is God **Glorified!**

His Glory. His prayer list.

His Glory, His Resume

GALATIANS 6:17 "...FOR I BEAR in my body the marks of Jesus."

II CORINTHIANS 11:23-26 "...BEEN IN prison more frequently, been flogged more severely, and been exposed to death again and again. Five times I received from the Jews the forty lashes minus one. Three times I was beaten with rods, once I was stoned, three times I was shipwrecked. I spent a night and day in the open sea, I have been constantly on the move, I have been in danger..."

II CORINTHIANS 12:7 "...THERE WAS given me a thorn in my flesh..."

II CORINTHIANS 12:9, 10 "...THEREFORE I will boast all the more gladly about my weaknesses so that Christ's power may rest on me. That is why, for Christ's sake, I delight in weaknesses, in insults, in hardships, in persecutions, in difficulties..."

II CORINTHIANS 12:11 "I HAVE made a fool of myself..."

ACTS 8:3 "BUT SAUL BEGAN to destroy the church. Going from house to house, he dragged off men and women and put them in prison."

What does God seek in a resume? What is on your resume if you have one? If not, what would you put on your resume if asked? Your education? Yes. Your accomplishments? Yes. Your qualifications? Yes. Your history? Yes. Your awards? Yes. Your achievements? Yes. Your personalized highlight film? Yes.

Would you mention prison time if you had spent time? Would you boast of your weaknesses? Would you call yourself a fool? Would you write down that you take delight in difficulties and insults? Would you discuss the marks on your body?

Paul's resume:

Been in prison frequently. Been flogged severely.

Five times I received the forty lashes minus one.

Three times beaten with rods.

Stoned once. Shipwrecked three times. Always on the move. Always in danger.

I boast of my weaknesses. I take delight in insults.

I take delight in hardships.

I take delight in persecutions. I take delight in difficulties.

I am a self-made fool.

I have marks on my body. I have a thorn in my flesh.

I sought to destroy the church.

I have gone house to house dragging off men and women to put them into prison.

Given his resume, would you have hired him? Would you have recommended him for a job? Do you know of any Fortune 500 company that would have hired him? Do you know of a church today that would have called him to lead their church or their children?

Then why did his resume qualify him to write about 25% of the New Testament in the Bible? In God's eyes, were the **marks** on his body "a requirement on the resume" before he could be approved to **mark** his words in His Holy Bible? **In God's eyes, were the marks on his body a visible resume of an invisible resume of a heart, mind, and soul totally yielded and committed to Him?** In God's eyes were his **marks** his identity in Christ? In God's eyes, were his marks meant to break him or make him? Or both?

A young girl, Lisa Fanning, was visiting the Yad Vashem Museum in Jerusalem with her parents. The museum is filled with photographs, letters, artifacts, and other numerous items of the Holocaust when six million Jews were murdered. There she saw the photographs of the dead as well as the malnourished men, women, and children, all with numbers tattooed on their wrists. Their **marks** of identity.

The next day her parents met a couple that had lived in the concentration camps and survived the Holocaust. As they were talking, her dad motioned her over to introduce her to this couple. When the man reached his arm out to shake her hand, her eyes became locked on the numbers tattooed on the man's wrist. She stared and stared and stared, and then looked up and said, "You're one of them." Yesterday's pictures had come alive. Yesterday's **marks** in a museum were today's **marks** in the flesh. The man's **marks** were the man's **resume.**

Any **marks** on your resume? Any **marks** of a submitted will? Any **marks** where you "fought the good fight"? (ll Timothy 4:7) Any **marks**, whether visible or invisible, to which someone could look at your life and say, "You're one of them"? **Marks** on your resume that make the words in the Bible come alive for others to see? Words studied in someone's Bible study of yesterday that became today's **marks** of His **Glory**?

In 1990, a man from the First Baptist Church of Caldwell, Texas, by the name of Ned McManus was killed in an accident on his farm.

At the funeral home the night before the service, his pastor, Reverend Phil Lovelace, was viewing the body and noticed **marks** on his arms and hands. He asked his son and daughter-in-law (Norris and Nadine), two very special committed Christians, how he received all the **marks.** They talked. He listened.

The next day at the funeral, Rev. Lovelace told the congregation about "the **marks**" during his eulogy. He said, "Mr. McManus had spent his last day on earth cutting a path for his grandkids, a shortcut to the lake. **Marks** of love. **Marks** of sacrifice. **Marks** of thoughtfulness. Always willing to cut a path for others to follow. Always willing to bear any **marks** in cutting that path. Visible **marks** on his body for cutting a path for his grandkids. Invisible **marks** in his heart for cutting a path for his Lord and Savior."

One day, when your resume is read as your obituary, will it include **marks** of eternal significance? Any **marks** from cutting new paths for your kids, grandkids, spouse, and friends? A new path of commitment? A new path of integrity? A new path of sacrifice? A new path seeking to **Glorify** the Lord?

Have the **marks** inflicted on you to cause you pain now become **marks** that reflect His Glory? Will the pastor at your funeral close with the words, "He (She) was one of them. How do I know this to be true? Because he (she) chose to bear the **marks** to bring God **Glory**. I saw the **marks**. I saw His **Glory**. His (her) marks, whether seen by man or only by God, were a resume of a life bringing God **Glory**."

His Glory. His marks. His resume.

His Glory, His Company

LUKE 23:32-43 "TWO OTHER MEN, both criminals, were also led out with Him to be executed. When they came to the place called The Skull, there they crucified Him, along with the criminals, one on His right, the other on His left. Jesus said, 'Father, forgive them, for they do not know what they are doing.' And they divided up His clothes by casting lots.

"The people stood watching, and the rulers even sneered at Him. They said, 'He saved others; let Him save Himself if He is the Christ of God, the Chosen One.'

"The soldiers also came up and mocked Him. They offered Him wine vinegar and said, 'If you are the King of the Jews, save yourself.'

"There was a written notice above Him, which read: This is the King of the Jews.

"One of the criminals who hung there hurled insults at Him: 'Aren't you the Christ? Save yourself and us!'

"But the other criminal rebuked him, 'Don't you fear God,' he said, 'since you are under the same sentence? We are punished justly, for we are getting what our deeds deserve. But this man has done nothing wrong.'

"Then he said, 'Jesus, remember me when you come into your Kingdom.'

"Jesus answered him, 'I tell you the truth, today you will be with me in paradise.'"

Three men. Three crosses. One man to a cross. One dying **in sin.** One dying **of sin.** One dying **for sin.**

The crowd. Those passing by hurl insults. So does His neighbor on the cross next to Him. The soldiers, chief priests, and teachers of the law will mock Him. The rulers sneer at Him. The disciples (except John) say nothing, because they aren't there.

The location. The place of the Skull (Golgotha in Aramaic).

The time. The third hour (9:00 a.m.) to the ninth hour (3:00 p.m.).

The picture. Jesus had been flogged. His back ripped open with a whip made of cords of leather intertwined with pieces of bone or metal. His face covered in blood due to a crown of thorns embedded in His head. Spikes of metal had been driven through His body into the cross. He was a bloody mess.

The view. One criminal on each side. Jesus sees both. Both see Jesus. Both see a beaten, battered, bloodied man gasping for breath. Both hear the insults. Both see the sneering. Both listen to the mocking.

The choice. One chooses to join in. He, too, adds his own insults to the Man in the middle. The other chooses to justify his own punishment, defends Jesus, and then asks Jesus to remember him in His kingdom. Jesus hears both.

The consequence. The one choosing to hurl insults will die **in sin,** and spend eternity without God and with others of like-minded hearts and souls who have also looked at Jesus and rejected Him. The one admitting his sin and asking Jesus to remember him in His Kingdom will die **of sin,** but will spend eternity in heaven with the One he asked to "remember me," the One in the middle, the One dying **for sin.**

The faith. Where did the sinner asking Jesus to "remember him" in His Kingdom receive his faith? What did he see that the other criminal didn't see? What did he hear that the other criminal didn't hear?

After all, **this was no picnic.** When he looked over to Jesus, he didn't see Him feeding 15,000 people with five loaves and two fish. He saw a man with a crown of thorns piercing His head and spikes driven through His body. **No miracle here.**

This was no boat ride. He wasn't on a boat with the disciples watching Jesus walk on water and still the storm. No, he was on a cross watching Jesus become still in death. **No miracle here.**

This was no wedding. He wasn't at Capernaum watching Jesus turn the water into red wine. No, he was on a cross watching the ground beneath Jesus turn red with His blood. **No miracle here.**

This was no mountainside. He wasn't there with the multitude hearing Jesus teach the Sermon on the Mount. No, he was on a cross hearing Jesus gasping for breath. **No miracle here.**

This was no transfiguration. He wasn't there with Peter, James, and John to see the face of Jesus shine like the sun. No, he was on a cross seeing the swollen face of Jesus, beaten and bruised. **No miracle here.**

This was no parade. He wasn't there to see Jesus riding into Jerusalem on a donkey with people laying down their palm branches while singing hymns of praise. No, he was on a cross, seeing people parade around Jesus, laying down their insults while shaking their hands and heads in mockery. **No miracle here.**

He saw no miracles, but then again, did he? When he looked into the eyes of Jesus, did he see more than eyes that were swollen, eyes squinting just to see, eyes revealing pain? **Did he see more,** did he see the miracle of eyes with compassion? Eyes of love? **Yes, a miracle here.**

Or was it what he heard? **Did he hear more** than the others? When he heard Jesus tell John, "Here is your mother," (John 19:27) did he hear the miracle of provision of a dying son to a grieving mother? **Yes, a miracle here.**

Or could it have been the words to those in mockery and insult, "Father, forgive them for they know not what they are doing"? Did he hear the miracle of forgiveness? **Did he hear more than forgiving words, did he hear the forgiving heart of God? Yes, a miracle here.**

Think about it. Did the criminal dying **of sin** hear and see the greatest miracles of Jesus? Do you think it ever crossed his mind as he was being nailed to the cross next to Jesus that he would spend that night in eternity with God?

We may not all be criminals, be we are all sinners. The question is, "Will we die **in sin** or **of sin?**" The answer depends on whether we believe Jesus died **for sin**, our sins. Once in heaven, I hope to find that criminal turned saint and ask him, "What did you hear and see that changed your eternal destiny?"

But more importantly, and getting personal, will we be able to ask someone in heaven one day, "What did you hear or see in my life that caused you to believe and change your eternal destiny?" Do you think it would be a view of us when we were on top of the world, or a view of us in humble adoration at the bottom? Do you think it would be hearing our words of wisdom or our words of forgiveness? Would it be a time they looked into our eyes and saw our heart, a heart of compassion and love reflecting our Lord?

Too often I am too busy and too selfish to see the needs of others. Several years ago, I was driving to work, behind schedule, and in a hurry. Suddenly, I noticed a lady on the other side of the road, standing in front of her car with the hood up and a red gas can on the ground beside her. I immediately thought, "She's on the other side of the road, not my responsibility. Someone else's turn to help." As I continued on my justified way, I looked back and saw no one had stopped. I said, "Lord, I don't have time for this, and I'm on the wrong side of the road going in a different direction." (As if He didn't know.) I slowed down still hoping someone on her side of the road would do the right thing and stop. I looked back one last time and saw no one had stopped yet. Then the Lord interrupted my pity party of excuses with the thought, "What if that helpless woman was your wife or your daughter? Would you want someone to stop and help them? Well, that helpless woman is someone's wife and someone's daughter, so…" I turned around and drove up right behind her van, her old van. She was a woman in her thirties, and very familiar with how to use her red gas can. I took her gas can to a nearby convenience store, filled it up with gas, and took it back to her van to empty it into her gas tank. I asked her to follow me to the convenience store to make sure everything was okay.

At the convenience store she went inside for a drink and I started filling her car up with gas. She came running out screaming, "No, no! I can't pay for all that gas. Please stop, please stop."

As I continued to fill up her car with gas, I quietly said, "Ma'am, don't worry. I'm paying for this and it is my privilege to do so." She began to cry and thank me. I quickly replied, "Please don't thank me, thank the Lord. This was His doing, not mine."

She continued crying for a couple of minutes and then said, "This is the first time in my life I have ever had a full tank of gas." That comment not only caught me off guard, but caught my attention as well and caused me to **look** at her differently, to **look** into her eyes wetted by tears of thankfulness and see a woman who God wanted me to stop and help.

She **looked** at me and said, "You were sent by God, weren't you?"

I said, "No, ma'am, I wasn't, but you were."

Why did more than a hundred cars on her side of the road pass her by and not stop? Because God wanted me to "look into her eyes and see His eyes." Her last words to me as she drove away were, "May God bless you."

I thought to myself, "Ma'am, He just did."

Three men. Three crosses. One man to a cross. The one dying **in sin** would miss the worship in eternal **Glory**. The one dying **of sin** would worship Him in eternal **Glory**. The One dying **for sin** would be worshipped in eternal Glory. Those to our left and those to our right are viewing us. What do they see? What do they hear? **Will they be there to worship Him in eternal Glory because they saw and heard us worship Him on earth for His Glory?**

His Glory. His view. Their view.

His Glory, His Brakes (Stop #1)

LUKE 18:35-43 "AS JESUS APPROACHED Jericho, a blind man was sitting by the roadside begging. When he heard the crowd going by, he asked what was happening. They told him, 'Jesus of Nazareth is passing by.'

"He called out, 'Jesus, son of David, have mercy on me.'

"Those who led the way rebuked him and told him to be quiet, but he shouted all the more, 'Son of David, have mercy on me!'

"Jesus **stopped** and ordered the man to be brought to Him. When he came near, Jesus asked him, 'What do you want me to do for you?'

"'Lord, I want to see,' he replied.

"Jesus said to him, 'Receive your sight; your faith has healed you.'

"Immediately, he received his sight and followed Jesus, praising God. When all the people saw it, they also praised God."

Think about it. Jesus never wondered what to do. Never thought, "What am I going to do today?" Through prayer, His paths were clear. He knew. But as He walked to where He knew to walk, no one in that walk ever became a nuisance, a bother, a distraction, or an inconvenience. **He knew that sometimes the interruption was the intended will of God.**

Jesus is walking to Jericho with a crowd following Him. A blind beggar couldn't see what was going on, but he sure heard the crowd, the noise, the excitement. He first asks what was happening. They tell him Jesus is passing by. He calls (shouts) out to Jesus to have mercy on him. The crowd rebukes him to **stop** the shouting, to be quiet. **He pays no attention to the crowd, none.** He then raises his voice even more and screams for mercy.

Then, Jesus stops. He puts on the brakes. The eternal God, the God of all creation, the God of the First and the Last, the God of Alpha and Omega, the God of Heaven and of Earth **stops** for a poor, penniless, blind beggar.

He, too, does not listen to the crowd and calls for the blind man to be brought to Him. As the man approaches Him, He asks the man what he wanted from Him. The blind beggar says he wants to see. He is then healed and immediately follows Jesus. The crowd, now with one more added to its ranks, all follow Him in praise.

Many years ago I heard a story about a seven-year-old blind boy who was placed inside a busy airport every weekend to help raise money for his family, whose father was very ill. He was put on a small stool, given a cup full of pencils in one hand, and an empty cup (with the word "Donation" written on it) in the other hand.

One Sunday, a man late for his plane was running through the airport with his head down, looking at his watch, and accidentally knocks the boy off his stool. Pencils scatter one way, the coins another way, and the little boy even another way. The man looked back at the boy, saw he wasn't hurt, looked at this watch, and kept running so as to not miss his flight.

Another man, on that same flight and not far behind, saw what happened, but he **stopped** to help the little boy. He picked up the little boy who had tears in his eyes, put him on his stool, and then picked up his pencils, his cups, and his coins. The man comforted the little boy and asked him if he is okay. The blind boy nodded his head, said he was fine, but then looked in the direction of the man and asked him, "Are you God?"

The man knelt down, took hold of the boy's hand, and said, "No, son, I'm not God, but I am one of His children."

The little boy, although unable to see, looked directly at the man and replied, "Well, sir, I knew you had to be some kind of kin." The man left to catch his flight with tears in his eyes, a lump in his throat, and a memory forever etched in his heart.

Two men. Same plane. Different destinations. Two men. Both late. One runs. One **stops.**

Two men. One picks up the pace. One picks up the pencils. Two men. One hears nothing. One hears a little boy ask him if he is God.

Two men. One sees a personal interruption. One sees divine intervention. Two men. One hits the accelerator. One hits the **brakes.**

Two men. One blinded by time. One blinded by tears. Two men. One took off. One took time.

Too often those that unexpectedly cross our paths at the most inconvenient of times can be seen as a bother, a hindrance to our rigid plans and tight schedules. Schedules that make no allowances or time for such interruptions.

In our busyness do we hear but not listen? In our rush do we look but not see? Does our hurry blind us? Do our lists bind us?

What if God listened to our prayers in the same way we listened to others? What if God gave us the time we give to others? And when life knocks us off our stool and everything in our world scatters, do you think Jesus would look at His watch and keep going?

Or would He **stop**, put on **His brakes**, put us back on our feet, and help pick up the pieces of our lives that have been scattered? If He **stopped** for a poor, penniless blind beggar, don't you think He would **stop** for you? He has already answered that question. If **His brakes** worked then, they will certainly work now. Maybe He is just waiting for you to call out. To cry out with no attention to the crowd.

Knowing that our Lord would **stop** for us as His children, do you think there are times He wants us to **hit the brakes and stop for others**? Looking back, maybe the only thing God wanted us to do that day, the one person who He purposely crossed our path to help, was the one person we did not make time for, the one person we considered to be an interruption. **Maybe the one person not on our list was the only person on God's list.**

Maybe God receives greater Glory through us when we aren't planning to do so. Those times when we see the interruption as His purposed intervention. Maybe the brightest light reflecting **His Glory** is the light coming from our **brake lights,** those times we **hit our brakes** for someone crossing our path at the most inconvenient of times**, a time when we did not consider them as a delay on our busy scheduled path, but as a divine detour for His greater Glory.**

No, not everyone crossing our path each day will be in need of us stopping to pick up their pencils. Not every interruption will be divine. But if our days remain too busy, if our lists become too long, and if our schedules stay too rigid, we may miss that one person crossing our path sent by God. That one person who might have asked us, "Are you one of God's children?"

His Glory. His pencils. His brakes.

His Glory, His Brakes (Stop #2)

LUKE **19:1-10** "JESUS ENTERED JERICHO and was passing through. A man was there by the name of Zacchaeus; he was a chief tax collector and was wealthy. He wanted to see who Jesus was, but being a short man he could not, because of the crowd. So he ran ahead and climbed a sycamore fig tree to see him, since Jesus was coming that way.

"When Jesus reached the spot, he looked up and said to him, 'Zacchaeus, come down immediately. I must stay at your house today.' So he came down at once and welcomed Him gladly.

"All the people saw this and began to mutter, 'He has gone to be the guest of a 'sinner.'

"But Zacchaeus stood up and said to the Lord, 'Look Lord! Here and now I give half of my possessions to the poor, and if I have cheated anybody out of anything, I will pay back four times the amount.'

"Jesus said to him, 'Today salvation has come to this house, because this man, too, is a son of Abraham. For the Son of Man came to seek and to save what was lost.'"

Earlier in the day, Jesus had **hit the brakes** and stopped for a poor, penniless, blind beggar. And now He **hits the brakes** and stops for a powerful, pocket-filled publican (a rich tax collector).

In Luke's version, the blind beggar had no name. The rich tax collector had one, Zacchaeus. The blind beggar had no money. Zacchaeus had plenty. The blind beggar was down and out. Zacchaeus was up and out. The blind beggar cried out loudly with all his might. Zacchaeus cried out silently with all his heart.

The blind beggar would have stayed blind had he continued sitting by the roadside. **He got up.** Zacchaeus would not have changed had he stayed in the tree. **He got down**. They both moved when called. They both moved in His direction. They both wanted to see. Jesus heard both. Jesus answered both.

One would look out for the first time. One would look in for the first time. The first person the blind beggar was ever to see was Jesus. The first person to ever see the person Zacchaeus could become was Jesus.

In the presence of Jesus, both changed their desires. The blind beggar was sitting by the roadside begging for food and money. When in the presence of Jesus, he asked for sight. Zacchaeus was sitting in a tree just wanting to see Jesus. When in the presence of Jesus, he volunteered to give up one half of his possessions and to make right for those times when he had cheated others. In His presence, their desires deepened. Their vision, clearer. Their hearts, more praiseful.

If Jesus were passing by you, would you cry out? Really cry out? If so, how? Soundly or silently? Would you let a crowd silence you? If Jesus stopped for you and said, "I must stay at your house today" (v. 5), what kind of home would He walk into? Would you ask Him the same thing in His presence as you do in your prayers? In His presence, would you thank Him more? Would you listen more intently?

In His presence, like Zacchaeus, do you think your conscience would cause more conviction? And with more conviction, more change? Do you think that in His presence you would see a reflection of the person He knows you can be, that person you so want to be? In His presence, do you think you would put away your "things to do list" and just enjoy being with Him, sharing with Him, and listening to Him?

I can't recall all the details, but years ago I heard a story about a father who wanted to spend time with his son, so he invited him to go camping over the weekend.

When they got back, the mom asked the son, "Well, how was your weekend? What all did you do? Did you catch a lot of fish? Did you go hiking? Did you have a good time?"

The son replied, "Mom, we didn't really do anything. No fishing. No hiking. We just sat around the fire talking, sharing, and laughing. I asked Dad a lot of questions and he gave me tons of things to think about. Mom, I had a great time, but I don't know if Dad did or not, because he is always on the go and we didn't do anything but talk."

Several months later the dad died in a car accident. A few weeks after the funeral the mom was going through some legal papers when she came across the dad's daily journal and planner. As she was going through it, she came across the camping weekend with their son. It read, "Went camping this weekend with John. It was the greatest two days I have ever spent with him. I loved listening to him. I loved laughing with him. I loved sharing with him and spending time with him. I loved just being with him. I love him as much as any father can love a son. Thank you, Lord, for this special time together."

When John came home from school, the mom showed him the journal and what his dad had written about the camping trip. With tears running down his cheeks, young John told his mom, "I knew Dad loved me, but I had no idea that he enjoyed me, and just enjoyed time with me and me alone."

Jesus spent more time in prayer with His Father than anyone who has ever lived. Can you imagine how much joy Jesus gave His Father by seeking so much time to be alone with Him, just the two of them. Father and Son. Father God and Son of Man.

Yes, Jesus **hit the brakes** and stopped for a blind beggar and a rich tax collector. The question is not will He **hit the brakes** and stop for us, but will we cry out for Him? Will we take the time to be alone with Him? Will we, as children of God, ever realize how much joy our heavenly Father receives in the time we spend with Him?

Yes, time in His presence will convict us. Yes, time in His presence will change us. Yes, time in His presence will chart us in new directions, new paths with new deepened desires to feed His sheep. Yes, time in His presence will bring Him great joy and even greater **Glory.**

His Glory. His brakes. His presence. His joy.

His Glory, His Room

REVELATION 3:20 "HERE I AM! I stand at the door and **knock…**"

LUKE 2:7 "…SHE WRAPPED HIM in strips of cloth and placed Him in a manger, because there was no **room** for them in the inn."

JOHN 8:37 "…YET YOU ARE ready to kill me, because you have no **room** for my word."

PSALM 10:4 "…IN ALL HIS thoughts there is no **room** for God."

He knocks. We hear. He knocks. We listen. He knocks. We consider. He knocks. We think. He knocks. We choose. He knocks. Do we open the door to invite Him in or do we not answer at all, sending Him away?

Does the door of our heart have a "No Vacancy" sign on it? Do we have room for His word? Do we have room for His thoughts? Do we have room for prayer? Do we have room for His will? Do we have room for Him?

Or are our lives just full? Our schedules secured. Our plans prioritized. Our days determined. Our calendars circled. Our time taken. Our paths planned. Our inn is full. The "No Vacancy" sign on our heart is brightly shining for all to see, including Him.

Dr. Buckner Fanning (who God used to bring me back from the far country about thirty years ago through his tape ministry with sermons of God's mercy and grace) tells the true story of a young boy from a small church in a small town south of San Antonio, Texas. We will call the young boy Tommy (yes, the same Tommy who gave Jesus his five loaves and two fish in another chapter) for this story.

For two years, the youth in this small church had put on a Christmas play for their church. Both years Tommy had done something, although unintentional, to turn a serious play into one of serious laughter.

Year one. Tommy is King Herod and sitting on his throne. The three wise men come before him, and as rehearsed, Tommy reaches down for his crown. **But** he mistakenly picks up the edge of the rug the wise men are standing on, thus causing the three wise men to lose their balance and fall to the floor. The crowd laughs.

Year two. Tommy is an angel with wings with nothing to pick up, nothing to say, nothing to do but just stand there. **But** Tommy is not one to stand for too long in one spot, so he begins to move ever so quietly, ever so slowly as to cause no notice. And then it happens. That last step takes him close enough to a burning candle to cause one of his angel wings to catch on fire, prompting Tommy to run all over the stage seeking to put out his fire. The crowd laughs again.

Year three. Several members of the youth group go to the teacher requesting that Tommy sit this year's Christmas play out, saying, "We want a serious play this year and Tommy will do something to ruin it just as he has the last two years. Please keep Tommy away."

The teacher responds, "I understand and can appreciate your request, but excluding Tommy would defeat the very meaning of Christmas. I'll give Tommy a small part with no wings and nothing to pick up."

So Tommy is given the part of the innkeeper with one line to say when Joseph knocks on the door. "I'm sorry, there is no room in the inn. Please go away."

At all the practices and rehearsals, Tommy says his one line to perfection. All other members of the youth group are taking notice, coming around to believing in him while still maintaining a justified skepticism.

It's the night of the play and all is going well just as the youth group desired. Now it is time for Tommy to say his one line. Joseph knocks on the door. Tommy opens the door and says, "I'm sorry there is no room in the inn. Please go away." Perfection! A perfect ten. The youth breathe a sigh of relief as the teacher smiles.

But as Joseph and Mary walk away from the inn, Mary begins to cry, something she had not done before in rehearsals. Tommy, seeing Mary in tears for the first time, yells out, "Stop, wait a minute, you can have my room!" The crowd laughs again. Another year, another Tommy.

The pastor was there to see the play that night, just as he had been the last two years. He knew Tommy's history, had seen what he had done, and heard not only what Tommy had said, but also the laughter of the crowd as well. He began to think and pray.

He began his sermon the next day talking about the play he had seen the night before, including what Tommy had said. The members of the congregation in the church laugh as Tommy slumps down in the pew to hide. He cannot believe his pastor has turned on him just like all the others.

But then the pastor says, "We need more men, women, and kids like Tommy. Too often I call some of you asking for help and your reply is just what the innkeeper said. 'I'm sorry, there is no room in my life, I'm already full, please go away.' There is always a 'No Vacancy' sign flashing with no time to share, no hands to help, no money to give, and no room for God. We need more people saying what Tommy said from his heart, 'Stop, wait a minute. You can have my time, you can have my talents, you can have my money, you can have me, Lord.' Thank you, Tommy, thank you."

Tommy cannot believe what he just heard and begins to straighten up in the pew. His shame has now been replaced with a smile. His view of the floor with head down has been replaced with a view of the entire church with his head held high. His words, "Stop, wait a minute, you can have my room," become words people rally around, much like many did years before with the words, "Remember the Alamo."

God uses the words of a child, touched by the tears of another child portraying the mother of Jesus, to start a revival in that church and town. People from different religions and different churches all begin to share and give of their time, talents, gifts, and money.

God choosing to be **Glorified** through the heart of a child, a child willing to give up "his room" for Jesus. God choosing to be **Glorified** through His Son, a son willing to give up "His room" in heaven to **Glorify** His father. Jesus leaving "His room" in heaven to take "His room" on the cross so we could have "room" in heaven. The cross was His and His alone, a "No Vacancy" sign visible for all to see. The cross was full: full of our sin, full of His love, and full of His **Glory.**

Is it time to answer His knocking on your heart?

Is it time to remove the "No Vacancy" sign on your heart?

Is His **Glory** one knock away?

Is His **Glory** one open heart away?

Is His **Glory** one "you can have my room" away?

Is His **Glory** one "you can have me, Lord," away?

His Glory. His knock. His room.

His Glory, His Flow Chart

JOHN 7:38, 39 "WHOEVER BELIEVES in Me, as the Scripture has said, streams of living water will **flow** from within him, By this He meant the Spirit…"

God's Spirit in us, designed to **flow** through us like streams of water **flowing** through the hillside. His Spiritual arteries **flowing** to our hearts to love as He would love, and to forgive as He would forgive. **Flowing** to our minds to think what He would think. **Flowing** to our hands to do what He would do, to our feet to walk where He would walk. **Flowing** to our eyes to see what He would see, to our cheeks to turn as He would turn.

An oasis within us, free **flowing** through us, calmly, continually, and quietly. We hear His soft voice. We feel His gentle touch. We follow His purposed path. We delight in His desires. We rest in His loving arms.

And then, we become busy. Busy in our work. Busy in our school. Busy in our home raising the kids. Busy in our volunteer work. Busy in our church. Busy, but a good busy.

And then, our good busy turns into "too busy." We rush. We hurry. Too busy to study. Too busy to pray. Too busy for others.

And then, something happens that may turn our world upside down and us inside out. We become discouraged. We become disappointed with others, ourselves, and especially God.

Discouragement leads to distance away from His word, away from prayer, away from Him.

And then, His Spirit within us, once free **flowing,** now becomes a faint trickle. The streams of living water have now been reduced to small roadside puddles created by isolated showers of prayer and study.

And then, there is blockage. His Spirit within us, seeking to **flow** through us with His Spiritual arteries, now finds blockage. He knocks, but we can't hear. He knocks, but we don't move.

About eighteen years ago, Dr. Mario Lammoglia (one of the top cardiologists in the country, a dear friend, and someone who God used to save my life not once, but twice) stood above my hospital bed and said with compassion, "Rob, you have heart disease. Your tests and **flow chart** show you have 85% to 95% blockage in five arteries reducing your blood **flow.** You need open heart surgery, and immediately."

Being the tough guy I am, I almost fainted. **And then,** the questions. How could I at the age of forty-six have heart disease? How could I have played golf a week ago, walking all eighteen holes carrying my bag, and have no symptoms, no signs? How could I have that much blockage and not know it? How? Why?

Two days later, thanks to the talent and skilled hands of Dr. James Kirby (a gifted Christian cardiovascular surgeon) my physical arteries were again **free flowing.**

And then, several months after surgery, the loving hand of God began His work on another set of arteries that remained blocked, my spiritual arteries. The Lord in His own way said, "Let's take a walk on the beach."

"Sounds like fun to me. I love the sound of waves crashing down on the sand. Let's go," I replied.

And then, I was to soon find out that my thoughts of a short, scenic stroll would turn into a long, painful journey. Now that my heart was free **flowing,** His voice was loud and clear. "Rob, as we walk along the beach, I want you to look at all the debris that has washed up on shore, debris that has come out of your heart, just yours. Debris that has clogged your spiritual arteries and blocked the **free flowing** of My Spirit in you." As I walked, I asked Him, "Did all this debris really come out of my heart?"

He replied, "Keep walking."

The walk continued with more and more debris littering the shoreline. I then said, "I didn't realize all that was in me."

Again He replied, "Keep walking."

Shortly, the surprise of all the debris so visible on the shoreline had turned into a deep sadness, now realizing the reasons for my spiritual blockage.

My spiritual arteries, blocked with too much pride and not free **flowing** with humility. Blocked with too much independence and not enough free **flowing** dependence. Blocked with too many answers and not enough free **flowing** questions. Blocked with too much credit for Rob and not enough free **flowing Glory** for the Lord, make that no **Glory** for Him. Blocked with too much of me and not enough of Him.

It took Dr. Kirby about four hours to finish his work on the operating table. It took the Lord several years just to begin His work on the beach, a work that is now going on eighteen years and counting. Waking up to the pain of having my chest cracked open to allow my physical arteries to free **flow** was no picnic, but nothing compared to the pain required by God's loving hands to remove the vast amount of debris blocking my spiritual arteries.

The process, painful. The purpose, priceless. As my spiritual arteries began to gradually open, His word became sharper. His voice, stronger. His burdens, lighter. His priorities, clearer. His fellowship nearer. His call for His **Glory,** brighter.

What about your heart? Your spiritual arteries? Is His Spirit free **flowing** in you? Any blockages?

Any debris? Any walks on the beach? Is He asking you to take a walk with Him on the shoreline?

If He is, go. Go now! Will it be painful? It has to be. Will it take longer than you might expect?

Probably. Will you want to stop and turn back? Absolutely. But keep going. Go!

And then, after your time on the beach seeing all that debris wash out of your heart, His Spirit, always in you, will once again start free **flowing** within you. Streams of living water **flowing** within you.

And then, slowly and surely, you will begin to hear His voice and feel His touch. Your **flow chart** will show His Spirit **flowing** through you, all of you. All your heart. All your body. All your mind. All your soul. And a Spirit that is **free flowing is a Spirit freeing up His Glory. All for His Glory.**

His Glory. His beach.

His Glory, His "Skin On"

JOHN 1:14 "THE WORD BECAME flesh and lived for a while among us."

The story is told of a young five-year-old little girl sound asleep late one night in her room.

Suddenly, a thunderstorm blows in with wind, rain, and lightning. A lightning strike near her home is accompanied by loud terrifying thunder.

The little girl is awakened and cries out for her father in the next room. The father rushes in to her room, sits on her bed, and holds his little angel in his arms. She says, "Daddy, I'm scared. Please stay in here with me tonight."

The father, sensing a good time to reinforce his teaching about God and his love, says, "Sweetie, God is here with us right now and He will watch over you and protect you."

She replies very softly, "Daddy, I know God is with us and watching over us, but tonight I need someone in here with 'skin on.'"

God knew, giving His creation a choice, that He would someday send His Son into the world with "skin on," skin that would be lashed with cords of leather and punctured with spikes of iron.

Of all the ways, of all the choices, of all the possibilities, He chose to save His creation of flesh with like flesh, flesh with "skin on." God, with "skin on," touching the lepers, touching those no one else would touch, touching the untouchables, a touching that would provide healing. (Matthew 8:3) God with "skin on," touching the blind, touching those no one could help, touching the hopeless, a touching that would provide sight. (Matthew 9:29, 30) God, with "skin on," touching the coffin of a mother's only son, touching death, a touching that would provide life. (Luke 7:14)

And then, God, with "skin on," allowing Himself to be touched by His creation. God, with "skin on," being touched by the tears of Mary and Martha, then weeping with tears of His own, tears of His flesh. (John 11:35) God, with "skin on," being touched with the hands of a woman with a blood disorder, a touching that healed her because of her faith. (Luke 8:44) God, with "skin on," asking Thomas to touch His side, a touching that would cause Thomas to say, "My Lord and my God," the only person in the New Testament to call Jesus God (John 20:28). God, with "skin on," telling all His disciples to touch Him, a touching that would help their unbelief and increase their faith. (Luke 24:39)

God, with "skin on," either touching His creation or being touched by them. A touch that brought healing. A touch that brought increased faith. A touch that brought new life.

Can God touch us today? Have you ever been touched by His forgiveness? By answered prayer?

What about a sunrise or a sunset? A beautiful rainbow? What about the birth of your child, did that touch you? What about the thought of Jesus dying on the cross for you and you alone, does that touch you?

But can we touch Him today? Jesus said in Matthew 25:37-40, "Then the righteous will answer him, 'Lord, when did we see you hungry and feed you, or thirsty and give you something to drink? When did we see you a stranger and invite you in, or needing clothes and clothe you? When did we see you sick or in prison and go to visit You?'"

"The King will reply, 'I tell you the truth, whatever you did for one of the least of these brothers of Mine, you did for Me.'"

My mother-in-law, Georgia Cummings, is as Christlike as anyone I've ever known. She is a woman of God. A woman of prayer. A woman touched by God. A woman touching others through God.

She visits the sick. She calls the lonely. She drives the disabled. She helps the elderly. She prays for the many. She encourages the discouraged. She listens to the broken. She gives to the lost. When in her presence, you feel you have been touched by God Himself. Can others say that about you? About me?

When we touch the hungry with food and the thirsty with water, we touch Him. When we touch a stranger with kindness, we touch Him. When we touch someone with needed clothes, we touch Him. When we touch the sick with needed help, or a visit to the hospital, we touch Him. When we touch a prisoner with a visit, we touch Him.

When we open our eyes, we see His **Glory.** When we open our hearts, others see His **Glory.**

When He touches us, we see His **Glory.** When we touch Him, others see His **Glory. It was His "skin on" that brought God to His creation. It will be our "skin on" that will bring others to our creator. And all for His Glory.**

His Glory. His touch.

His Glory, His Mr. Israeli Contest

I Samuel 16:3 "...you are to anoint for me the one I indicate."

I Samuel 16:10-12 "Jesse had seven of his sons pass before Samuel, but Samuel said to him, 'The Lord has not chosen these.' So he asks Jesse, 'Are these all the sons you have?'
'There is still the youngest,' Jesse answered, 'but he is tending the sheep...'
Then the Lord said, 'Rise and anoint him; he is the one.'"

John 6:63 "...the flesh counts for nothing"

Matthew 5:14 "You are the light of the world."

Matthew 5:16 "In the same way, let your light shine before men, that they may see your good deeds and praise your Father in heaven."

While David is tending to the sheep, a "Mr. Israeli" contest is going on in his home. The Lord has told Samuel to go to Jesse of Bethlehem to choose one of his sons to be king. So Jesse brings out seven of his sons, each one flexing his muscles in different poses of earthly flesh and power. Seven sons take center stage to strut their stuff, and seven times God says no to their outward display of worldly attributes.

Jesus said, "…The flesh counts for nothing." (John 6:63) Not some, nothing. Not one percent, zero.

Adam Redpath put it this way, "The perfection of the flesh is always rejected in heaven."

Man looks outside. God looks inside.

Man measures the size of houses. God measures the size of hearts. Man says, "Elevate thyself." God says, "Deny thyself."

After Samuel had witnessed this earthly parade of earthly power pass before him, he asks Jesse, "Are these all the sons you have?" (My translation: "Did I miss something, is this it?")

Jesse replies, "There is still the youngest, but he is tending the sheep." (My translation: "I have one more son tending to the sheep, but I can assure you if you didn't approve of any of these stallions, you're sure not going to approve of this little pony in the field.") Jesse took no thought of even inviting his young shepherd son to take part in the "Mr. Israeli" contest for he (David) did not look the part, not at all.

Many years ago, I told the Lord, "I will never hire a Christian again." I had been burned too many times by those saying the right things, those looking the part, those qualified to enter and win any "Mr. Israeli" or "Mr. America" contests because of their showroom qualities. Enough was enough. No more tire tracks. No more Christians.

Lee Corso would have answered, "Not so fast, my friend," but God answered by sending a Mr. Willis to talk to me about his son, Lee. God put it this way, "I have one more for you to look at before you make your final decision on not hiring any more of My children. He is a young pastor who has been 'tending My sheep' in a small church not far from here. He, too, has had a bad experience with some of the sheep in that church who were seeking one who could win a "Mr. Israeli" contest, and he just didn't measure up. And although he didn't meet their expectation, he has won My heart with his humility, meekness, gentleness, and kindness. He is a man of God with My heart and My spirit, and he will never hurt you or harm you. He needs you and you need him."

A short time later, and true to his word, God sent a young, beaten pastor through the front door of our restaurant. His name, Lee Willis. His spirit, sweet. His hands, open. His touch, gentle. His voice, soft. His words, kind. His heart, all God's.

No, there was not much muscle there to flex. No, there was not much strut in his stride. But then again, he had no desire for either. For Lee was not a man seeking after muscle or might, but was a man after God's own heart, a man seeking to **Glorify** the Lord.

As I recall, Lee worked with us for about a year, with each and every day bringing forth a fresh supply of God's love, God's mercy, and God's grace. Did God use Lee to change my mind about "never hiring Christians" again? Absolutely. But God brought Lee into my life for much more than to renew my hiring practices. God used Lee to help "renew a right spirit within me." God revealed through Lee a number of "Mr. Israeli" contests of my own. Contests of earthly pursuit. Contests of worldly passions. Contests of standards of success. Contests of secular strut.

Jesus said, "You are the light of the world." (Matthew 5:14) "In the same way, let your light shine before men, that they may see your good deeds and praise your father in heaven." (Matthew 5:16) The light of God, shining through Lee, revealed the darkness of the many "Mr. Israeli" contests I was seeking to win and allowed God to renew a right spirit within me.

Do you have any "Mr. Israeli" contests of your own? Contests where your light is a spotlight on you and your desires at center stage rather than reflecting your light to what God is seeking? Are you spending your days seeking the crowns of the "Mr. Israeli" contests to which you have entered, or are you seeking the crowns that bring God **Glory**?

Are you a light shining in the darkness of others, a light of such humility and meekness that it brings conviction and repentance in the lives of others, which brings God **Glory**? This "light of the world" is not one held in our hand as a spotlight in judgment, but as a light in our heart reflecting and illuminating the **Glory** of God from within us.

His Glory. His crown. His light.

His Glory, His Attire

I Samuel 17:4–6 "A champion named Goliath, who was from Gath, came out of the Philistine camp. He was over nine feet tall. He had a bronze helmet on his head and wore a coat of scale armor of bronze weighing five thousand shekels [about 125 pounds], on his legs he wore bronze greaves, and a bronze javelin was slung on his back."

I Samuel 17:8 "Goliath stood and shouted to the ranks of Israel."

I Samuel 17:16 "For forty days the Philistine came forward every morning and evening and took his stand."

I Samuel 17:24 "When the Israelites saw the man, they all ran in great fear."

I Samuel 17:38, 39 "Then Saul dressed David in his own tunic. He put a coat of armor on him and a bronze helmet on his head. David fastened on his sword over the tunic and tried walking around, because he was not used to them. 'I cannot go in these,' he said to Saul, 'because I am not used to them.' So he took them off."

I Samuel 17:47 "All those gathered here will know that it is not by sword or spear that the Lord saves; for the battle is the Lord's and He will give all of you into our hands."

Ephesians 6:11 "Put on the full armor of God so that you can take your stand against the devil's schemes."

Ephesians 6:13 "Therefore, put on the full armor of God, so that when the day of evil comes, you may be able to stand your ground, and after you have done everything, to stand."

David vs. Goliath. A familiar story of a little shepherd boy versus a nine-foot giant. A favorite story of many children and adults alike. A factual story of an underdog who didn't stand a chance against a giant who stood so large.

Can you picture this giant of a man, with his bronze armor glistening in the sun, hurling unanswered insults and taunts to the men of Israel, the children of God? For forty days he ran his mouth, and for forty days they ran in fear. A pathetic picture of His children on the run. But are we, too, His children still on the run?

Today, Goliath is not just one man clothed in bronze battle gear taunting the children of God.

No, today there are many Goliaths clothed in modern-day garb and attire, walking throughout our country. Like Goliath, they run their mouths and are loud. The have gained ground through our compromising and fears.

It was my first year to play Little League baseball. I was eight years old and a pitcher on our team, a good team that was in first place. It was a normal Saturday morning and all was going well as usual. I went out to the mound to pitch the last inning, to give our team another victory, but then it all changed. The other team started calling me names, making fun of me, and laughing at me. This had never happened to me before, never. I looked over to their dugout and they yelled even louder and laughed even harder. Tears rolled down my cheeks while I stood motionless staring at the ground. My dad, an assistant coach, comes out to the mound, his first and only trip of the season.

I wipe away a few tears, look up to him, and say, "Dad, I didn't do anything to them. I didn't say anything to them. Why are they making fun of me and laughing at me?"

He doesn't answer my questions, but he tells me in a loving voice, "Rob, you have a choice to make. You can walk off the mound with me and go back to the dugout, or you can look 'em in the eye, smile at 'em, and beat 'em with your best. Either way, you're my son, I love you, and I will be proud of you."

Dad didn't tell me what to do. He knew what he wanted me to do, but he knew it needed to be my decision. He gave me a choice "to run from them" or "to stay and face them." But with that choice came an assurance of his love, an unwavering love that never changed with my choices.

I looked up at his smiling face and said, "I'll stay, smile at them, and throw my best at them." As soon as my dad walked back to the dugout, the other team continued their name-calling and laughter. I looked over one last time, smiled, and struck out the last three hitters. We won the game, but the victory belonged to Dad.

Maybe to this day that is why the story of "David and Goliath" is one of my all-time favorites, because Dad taught me to "face" my Goliaths and not "run" from them. To look my Goliaths in the eye and not blink. To stand firm and not budge. And to turn the insults and laughter of the Goliaths into victories for the Lord.

When it was time for David to battle Goliath, Saul dressed David in his own tunic, coat of armor, and bronze helmet, all resembling the armor of Goliath minus a few sizes. David tried them on, then took them off, and then said in his own way, "This just isn't me. This doesn't wear well. This doesn't fit." **David knew the armor of Goliath was not the armor of God. David knew it was no use trying to imitate the enemy, to look like he looked, to wear what he wore, to stand where he stood, and to trust in what he trusted.** So David answered Goliath's boasts and cursing with these words, "You come against me with sword and spear and javelin, but I come against you in the name of the Lord Almighty, the God of the armies of Israel... All those gathered here will know that it is not by sword or spear that the Lord saves, for the battle is the Lord's and He will give all of you into our hands."(1 Samuel 17:45-47) **David also knew** it was of no use in fighting like the enemy, with his words, with his ways, and with his weapons. He knew he could not fight the battle on his terms, on his level, and on his own.

Goliath looked down at David. David looked up to God. Goliath hurled his insults. David hurled his stone. And then it was over. David's victory over Goliath was a victory for the children of God, a victory bringing **Glory** to God.

Can you recognize a Goliath when you see him, hear him, or read what he writes? Have you allowed the Goliaths of the world that come in all different shapes and sizes to silence you or possibly even shame you? Have you been retreating, on the run? Have you tried to imitate him, to blend in as not to stand out or be noticed?

Or are you standing firm, facing your Goliaths in the name of the Lord? Are you allowing God's Spirit to flow within you to conquer and down your Goliaths for His **Glory**? Can others see you are clothed in His righteousness, in His attire, and have not one stitch of the world's apparel?

But know this. The courage you show in facing your Goliaths, and the determination you display in seeking to defeat your Goliaths, will bring **Glory** to God.

His Glory! His battles! His victories!

His Glory, His Stone Ezel

KING SAUL AND ALL HIS men are in great fear, running **away** from Goliath. David runs **toward** the battle, steps up, and with one stone from a handmade slingshot, takes Goliath out. One Goliath. One David. One prayer. One stone. One dead giant. One hero. Saul's fear of Goliath becomes a victory for David. Later, Saul's fear of David will become a victory for Israel, and **Glory** for the Lord.

The Victory Parade

1 SAMUEL 18:6 "WHEN THE men were returning home after David had killed the Philistine, the women came out from all the towns in Israel to meet King Saul with singing and dancing, with joyful songs and with tambourines and lutes."

After defeating Goliath and the Philistines, the women came out from all over Israel singing songs and rejoicing in the streets. Victory parties. Victory parades. Victory confetti. Victory speeches. Victory songs. Victory smiles.

The Victory Song

1 Samuel 18:7 "Saul has slain his thousands, David his tens of thousands."

This song giving David more credit and more praise becomes a sour note in Saul's ear, a jealous irritation in Saul's eye and an evil spirit in Saul's heart. All these combined will put a spear in Saul's hand.

The Contract

1 Samuel 19:1 "Saul told his son Jonathan and all the attendants to kill David."

1 Samuel 19:9, 10 "While David was playing the harp, Saul tried to pin him to the wall with his spear."

1 Samuel 19:11 "Saul sent men to David's house to watch it and to kill him in the morning."

The success of David, the fear of David, and his jealousy of David all lead to a "contract" on David. Saul has had enough and puts a "contract" out on David's life.

The Friend

1 Samuel 18:1 "After David had finished talking with Saul, Jonathan became one in spirit with David."

God provides a needed friend for David. His name is Jonathan, son of Saul, the King who has just issued the contract on his life. Jonathan and David are one in spirit, one in trust, and one in heart.

The Plan

1 Samuel 19:2, 3 "My father Saul is looking for a chance to kill you. Be on your guard tomorrow morning; go into hiding and stay there. I will go out and stand with my father in the field where you are. I'll speak to him about you and will tell you what I find out."

1 Samuel 20:19-20 "...wait by the **Stone Ezel.** I will shoot three arrows to the side of it, as though I was shooting at a target."

Jonathan will talk to his father about David, to seek answers about David's safety. And while Jonathan talks, David will wait and wait. He will wait until Jonathan shoots an arrow, an arrow that will determine his direction in life. An arrow landing before him will mean all is safe and all is well to come back home. An arrow beyond him will mean he must go away. Away from home. Away from Jonathan. Away from friends. Away from the known, and away to the unknown. Away to uncertainty. Away to confusion. Away to doubts. Away to questions, many questions.

The Stone

1 Samuel 20:19 "…and wait by the Stone Ezel."

David is waiting by the Stone Ezel, waiting for direction, waiting for an answer. Think about the questions he might have been asking, the thoughts he might have been thinking. How did I get here? All I did was **obey**. I left my sheep to **obey** my father. I left home to **obey** Saul. I left a nine-foot giant dead to **obey** my Lord. And now I am left to just wait. I am left without one thing I can do to choose my direction, my path. I am left with no choice, no say, and no answers.

The Arrow

1 Samuel 20:37 "When the boy came to the place where Jonathan's arrow had fallen, Jonathan called out after him, 'Isn't the arrow beyond you?'"

1 Samuel 20:41 "…and wept together, but David wept the most."

David is waiting. He hears Jonathan's voice. The time is now. His direction soon determined.

Jonathan shoots the arrow and it keeps going and going and going. Beyond him. Imagine the lump in his throat. The pounding in his heart. The tears on his cheeks. His wait is now over. His direction is now determined. His compass now set. And unknown to him, God had used Jonathan to give him the direction he needed in preparation for the throne.

God placed Jonathan in David's life. David had no one. David needed someone. Jonathan was that someone. They were one in spirit. Do you have a Jonathan in your life? Someone always there for you? Someone you completely trust? Someone willing to sacrifice so much for you? Someone who believes in you? Someone who prays for you? Someone God has placed in your life? Are you a Jonathan in someone's life?

Dr. Curtis Garrett is that Jonathan in my life. A truly gifted oral and maxillofacial surgeon, one of the best in the country and a true disciple of Christ. Curtis has been, is, and will always be there for me, an anchor during my darkest hours. A true friend. A real Jonathan, giving direction as I waited by my "Stone Ezel."

Can you recall a **time** and **place** in your life where you were waiting by your "Stone Ezel"? Just waiting. You said all there was to say, done all there was to do, and prayed all there was to pray. Nothing left in you. Maybe no one by you. Emptied and waiting. Emptied and anxious.

A **time** of waiting. A **place** you did not choose. A **time** of questions. A **place** of helplessness. A **time** of "whys." A **place** of crossroads. But also, unknown to you, a **time** and **place** of God's hand and leading.

Are you there now? Perhaps your wait is for a phone call from your doctor with results of the biopsy or blood work. A benign arrow before you will keep you at home. A cancerous arrow beyond you will take you away, away to the unknown of treatments and hospitals. Perhaps you're in a hospital now, awaiting the results of a loved one's surgery. Perhaps your wait is for a letter in the mail. An admission or rejection letter from the university you are seeking to attend. A letter from an attorney, with divorce papers attached. A letter from your employer, possibly relocating you to another part of the country or terminating your services.

But this is your "Stone Ezel," not David's. This is your stone, personalized with your name on it.

This is your heartbeat that quickens. This is your breath that deepens. This is your wait, your future. Then the phone rings, the letter arrives. Your wait is over. Your answer has now come.

Like all of us, I have waited by that "Stone Ezel" many times. I've come to realize "the arrows" come in different shapes, sizes, speeds, and significance. Some arrows may determine a course study in college while some may determine a course of treatment for a serious sickness. Some arrows come slowly and test our patience while some come quickly and test our preparation. Some arrows may bring a smile to our face while some may bring a sting to our sadness.

I had just taken the LSAT, the Law School Admittance Test, and told Susan, my new bride of several months, that I thought I had done really well on the test. So as I waited by my "Stone Ezel" for the test results, I started looking at all the law schools that interested me. I waited and waited, and finally the letter arrived in the mail. I quickly opened the letter with great anticipation and expectation. The wait now over as I read my test score, bottom 10% of the nation. God had sent the letter airmail and sent it so far beyond me that it erased any future thought of law school. Back to the "Stone Ezel."

So I quickly started the interview process with different companies at the career center at Texas A&M University. Shortly thereafter, I received a telephone call from "Mr. Smith" representing a company in Ft. Worth, Texas. He wanted me to come to Ft. Worth for an interview with him and other company personnel.

I make the trip to Ft. Worth and he offered me a job at the end of the day. I tell "Mr. Smith" I'm excited and thankful, and would like to discuss this with my wife and pray about it. He agreed and tells me to call him in five days.

So Susan and I pray and wait by the "Stone Ezel" for direction, for an answer. Do we go or not go? Is this God's will? Is His arrow coming from Ft. Worth? We pray, we seek, and we wait. On about the fourth day, the wait is over. I receive a phone call from another representative of the company telling me "Mr. Smith" was no longer with the company and my employment offer had been withdrawn. Yes, God's arrow had come from Ft. Worth and was sent beyond me again. Back again to that "Stone Ezel," which was becoming all too familiar. Back again for more waiting, for more arrows.

Sometimes the arrow is before us and all is well. Sometimes the arrow is beyond us and all will change with all new paths. **Sometimes His answers and the paths of His choosing** run contrary to the paths **of our planning.** Sometimes His arrows take us in a different direction than our desires. Like David, sometimes His arrows are sent beyond us to prepare us and to strengthen us for God's greater **Glory.**

But by knowing that our personalized arrows have come from the hand of God as a symbol of the will of God and for the purpose of the Glory of God, we can stand in faith by our "Stone Ezel" in confident expectation of the goodness and love of God.

His Glory. His stone. His arrow.

His Glory, His View of Black and White

LUKE 18:9-14 "TO SOME WHO were confident of their own righteousness and looked down on everybody else, Jesus told this parable: 'Two men went up to the temple to pray, one a Pharisee and the other a tax collector. The Pharisee stood up and prayed about himself; 'God, I thank you that I am not like all other men—robbers, evildoers, adulterers—or even like this tax collector. I fast twice a week and give a tenth of all I get.'

"But the tax collector stood at a distance. He would not even look up to heaven, but beat his breast and said, 'God, have mercy on me, a sinner.'

"I tell you that this man, rather than the other, went home justified before God. For everyone who exalts himself will be humbled, and he who humbles himself will be exalted."

I love the stories of Jesus. So many, like this one, give us contrasts, choices, and consequences of those choices. His parables are timeless, meant for those who heard it then and those of us who read it now.

This is a story of two men and two prayers. One stood up. One stood back. One looked up in pride. One looked down in humility. One gave his credentials **to** God. One cried for mercy **from** God. **One gave God his resume. One gave God his heart. One would be dignified. One would be justified.**

Which of the two men can you identify with and relate to? An easy choice, right? But what if the Lord were to ask you, "Are there any sins in your life that you have rationalized to be right? Sins of dignity? Sins of reason? Sins no longer called sins?"

Many years ago, a young pastor from Caldwell, Texas, told me about a man coming to his office to have his dream interpreted. He told the man he wasn't a psychologist and couldn't help him. The man insisted on telling him his dream, a dream so real it kept him up all night. The young pastor agreed to listen.

The man began, "A small dim light led me into this dark, damp room filled with black monuments of different shapes and sizes. The room was cold, dismal, and made me feel very uncomfortable. It was difficult to see, but I saw enough as to want out. Then this light took me out of that room and into another. This room was beautiful and bright, filled with both white and crystal monuments that glistened in all the light. The room was warm, cozy, and comfortable. The monuments were pleasing to the eye. I wanted to stay, but the light took me out to show me the back of a man, a back bloodied from a beating and scourging. So pastor, what do you think?"

The young pastor wisely replied, "As I said, I don't interpret dreams, I teach and preach God's word, but here is what it means to me. The dark room with black monuments, those could be sins in your life, dark sins you know to be wrong. Sins you have confessed to God. Sins as black as night and as cold as ice. Monuments making you feel uncomfortable, a darkness demanding your exit. You wanted out.

"Then this light, the light of God, led you into the next room. This room, with all the beautiful white and crystal monuments that reflected in all the light, was a room of warmth, all things pleasing to the eye. You were comfortable. You wanted to stay.

"Maybe those beautiful white and crystal monuments are the sins in your life you have rationalized to be right. You are comfortable with those sins. You have turned black monuments of sin into white monuments of accepted behavior. You have turned white lies into white monuments. You have turned wrong sin into right sin. You have turned dark sin into dignified sin.

"And then the light of God took you out to see the back of a Man who had been scourged, the back of Jesus. Christ Jesus, the Man whose blood has already covered your black monuments, but whose blood has yet to leave a crimson stain on your white monuments. All monuments, whether black or white, require the crimson blood of Jesus."

Do you have any white monuments? Monuments that glisten with rays of rationalized sin? Monuments you have reasoned to be right? Monuments in the privacy of your mind? Monuments of ownership? Monuments untouched thus far by the blood of Jesus? Monuments that may even have a comfortable place in your heart?

We must be careful that the light glistening from our white monuments does not blind us from the light of God seeking to reflect His Glory through us. Jesus said, "You are the light of the world.... In the same way, let your light shine before men, that they may see your good deeds and praise your Father in heaven." (Matthew 5:14-16)

Two men. One dignified. One justified. The one dignified would not be justified before God. The one justified would not be dignified before God.

Our light, always visible for others to see, will either glisten from our dignified collection of white monuments, or shine before men in humble adoration, **Glorifying our Lord.**

His Glory. His light.

His Glory, His "One"

JOHN 1:14 "THE WORD BECAME flesh and lived for a while among us. We have seen His Glory, the Glory of the One and only Son…"

JOHN 1:26, 27 "I BAPTIZE with water," John replied, "but among you stands One you do not know. He is the One who comes after me, the thongs of whose sandals I am not worthy to untie."

JOHN 1:29, 30 "THE NEXT day John saw Jesus coming toward him and said, 'Look, the Lamb of God who takes away the sins of the world! This is the One…'"

MATTHEW 11:2 "WHEN JOHN HEARD in prison what Christ was doing, he sent his disciples to ask Him, 'Are you the One who was to come, or should we expect someone else?'"

MATTHEW 3:12 "HIS WINNOWING FORK is in His hand, and He will clear His threshing floor, gathering the wheat into His barn and burning up the chaff with unquenchable fire."

John looks at Jesus and says, "You're the One." The One he had been praying for. The One he had been preparing for. The One he had been preparing others for. The One he had been looking for. Not One of two. Not One of many. One of One. The One. All those years of waiting, of preaching, of preparing. And then his eyes lay hold of Jesus. He knew. The wait now over. The anticipation ended. The heart pounding. The Lamb of God cometh. The prayers answered. The One and only Son of God before him. This is the One...

Susan and I were married in August of 1973. That December we went to visit my parents for Christmas, and I vividly remember a conversation I had with my dad. It went something like this.

"Rob, I've been around Susan long enough to know two things. One, you over-married." I asked, "What does that mean?"

He answered, "I'll put this in terms you can understand. You're minor league. She's major league. Understand now?"

As I saw the grin on his face I replied, "I totally agree, but I didn't realize it was that obvious."

He then said, "Secondly, I knew she was the one I had been praying for when I first met her."

I then asked, "And how did you know she was the one before I knew she was the one?"

Dad answered, "Because she was the one God used to bring life into your living. Her zeal for life was contagious and you began to live, truly live. Right away I knew she was the one I had been praying for."

Five years later, I started praying for our kids (Robby and Callie) the minute Susan told me she was pregnant with them. Praying first for their salvation, that they would trust in Jesus as their Lord and Savior. Secondly, I began praying for their spouses, the **one** person God was preparing for them, to complete them, to honor Him.

About twenty-five years after his birth, our son Robby called and said he was bringing home his girlfriend Katie for the weekend. Susan told me she believed Katie was the **one**, and because her instincts were always right, I started waiting in great anticipation. Robby called us that Friday afternoon and said they are about ten minutes away. I then began to pace, look out the window, pace, look out the window, pace...

They drove up and Robby opened the door for Katie. She got out of the Tahoe and my eyes saw her for the first time. I remember thinking, "So you're the one, the **one** I was praying for three years before you were born. The one I was praying for when only God knew of your coming birth. Twenty-five years of praying now answered in the life before me. So you're the **one**..."

Several years later that same scenario took place again when Tony asked our daughter Callie to marry him. Then looking at him like I had looked at Katie, and thinking, "Twenty-four years of praying and "you're the **one**."

Based on my feelings of joy and thankfulness when I first saw Katie and Tony, and knowing they were the "ones," I can only imagine what John the Baptist was feeling and thinking when he first saw Jesus, knowing He was the One he had been praying for, the One he had been preparing for, and the One he had been preparing others for.

I can only imagine what John thought when he looked at Jesus and saw the One person who could and would take away the sins of the world.

I can only imagine John looking into the eyes of Jesus knowing he was looking into the eyes of God.

I can only imagine how John felt knowing God had revealed to him the "Lamb of God" but not to the religious leaders of the day.

Then I can only imagine why John, once so sure of Jesus being the One, the Lamb of God, became so unsure in his belief.

I can only imagine that maybe his confinement in prison caused him some doubt.

I can only imagine that possibly he was expecting the Messiah, the Lamb of God who would take away the sins of the world, to also take over the world. Maybe with might? Possibly with power? But for sure, a conquering Messiah.

I can only imagine what he was thinking when he was in prison and sent two of his followers to ask Jesus, "Are you the One who was to come, or should we expect someone else?"

Could John have been thinking, "Was I wrong in saying you were the One? Where is your army? Your followers? Your power? Your takeover? You are not acting like I thought you would act. You are not doing what I thought you would do. You are not carrying the winnowing fork I thought you would carry. You are not burning up the chaff with unquenchable fire I thought you would burn. I was once so sure you were the One, but now I have my doubts, I just don't know anymore. I'm confused. Are you the One?"

I can only imagine that his doubts were caused by his expectations of Jesus not being answered by the actions of Jesus, or the lack of actions of Jesus.

I can only imagine the anticipation of John's followers after they asked Him if He was the One.

I can only imagine that they expected a simple "yes" or "no" answer from Jesus. But a simple answer they did not receive. For any simple person with any simple ego could have answered, "Yes." A false prophet could have said, "Yes." A self-anointed, self-appointed Messiah could have said, "Yes." John wanted "yes" or "no," but Jesus gave him more, much more. Sometimes in reading the Bible it is important to not only read what was written or said, but what was not written or said. In this case, it is important to note what Jesus didn't say in His answer to John's disciples. No mention of an army. No mention of a takeover. No mention of riding a white horse while conquering the world. No mention of a simple "yes." And no mention of any plans to free him from prison.

Here was the reply of Jesus: "Go back and report to John what you hear and see. The blind receive sight, the lame walk, those who have leprosy are cured, the deaf hear, the dead are raised, and the good news is preached to the poor. Blessed is the man who does not fall away on account of me." (Matthew 11:4-6)

His reply to John's disciples was one that could have only been answered by the One. For only the One and only Son of God, the Lamb of God, could give the blind their sight, the deaf their hearing, the lepers their new skin, the lame their new legs, and the dead their new life.

Maybe He was telling John, "I know I'm not doing what you expected Me to do. And maybe I'm not the kind of Messiah you expected Me to be. And maybe I'm not using My power like you expected Me to use it. But, John, listen to Me, really listen to My words. I am using My power to Glorify God. Every person I heal, every person I raise from the dead, every word I share with the poor, and everything I do is to bring Glory to God in the path of His choosing. His Glory, His way."

And then Jesus closes with these words, "Blessed is the man who does not fall away on account of Me." (Matthew 11:6). Is He saying to John, "God used you to prepare a path for Me and you did it well. Now don't let your expectations of Me become a stumbling block because of God's instructions and expectations of Me. John, you began well, now finish well. Don't fall away now."

Have you expected God to act in a certain way and He didn't? Have you ever sent word to God in prayer asking Him, "Are you the One? Are you sure this is your will?" Have you ever been so sure of God and then become so unsure of Him because He didn't act like you expected Him to act? Or He didn't seem to act at all? Have your expectations of God ever come crashing down? Have you ever thought you knew Him and His ways, only to find out differently? Have unanswered expectations of God become a stumbling block in your path to reflect His Glory? Has your stumbling block caused a stumbling block for others? Like John, so often our misguided expectations of God can take us to our place of confinement, our own prison. And no, we don't have to be behind bars to be in bondage. **So often we imprison ourselves when our expectations of Him and from Him exceed our adoration and Glory for Him.**

Sometimes there is a great joy in seeing God answer a prayer of twenty-five years. And yes, sometimes there is a great disappointment in seeing God act differently than we expected. But just as His blood covers all our sins, His Glory covers all our doubts, all our questions, and all our misguided expectations.

His Glory. His Way.

His Glory, His Lack of Memory

ISAIAH 43:25 "I, EVEN I, am He who blots out your transgressions for my own sake, and remember your sins no more."

JEREMIAH 31:34 "FOR I WILL forgive their wickedness and will remember their sins no more."

ISAIAH 44:22 "I HAVE SWEPT away your offenses like a cloud, your sins like the morning mist."

PSALM 103:12 "...AS FAR AS the east is from the west, so far has He removed our transgressions from us."

COLOSSIANS 2:13, 14 "HE FORGAVE us all our sins, having canceled the written code, with its regulations, that was against us..."

REVELATION 21:4 "HE WILL WIPE away every tear from their eyes."

God created us with a memory. We have the memory of loved ones, special times, dear friends. The list could go on and on. Part of our memory serves to protect us from harm, pain, and injury. If we touch a fire once, our memory tells us "Don't touch that again." If someone hurts us and causes us great pain, our memory tells us to "Keep your distance," "Keep your guard up" and "Watch your back." We can forgive, but not forget. Our memory protects us from further pain, further hurt, and further disappointment. We say, "Hurt me once, shame on you. Hurt me twice, shame on me." So often our memory tells us to move back, to move on, or to even move out.

But the God who created His creation with a memory, chose to not have one concerning our confessed sins. He chose to not only forgive our sins, but forget them as well. God choosing to remember our sins no more, putting Himself in His relationship with us to be hurt over and over again. And many times for the same sin day after day. But by choosing to "remember our sins no more," there is never any distance between us. No walls. No barriers. No "guards up." No moving back. No moving out.

A woman in a hospital needed surgery. She had no family. No friends. She sat on her hospital bed staring straight ahead, oblivious to all. She would not respond to nurses or doctors. No one. A doctor, fearful of performing the surgery she needed because of her mental state, called a local pastor, Dr. Buckner Fanning, for help.

Dr. Fanning responded right away and came into her room. He gave her his best counseling, best encouragement, and read selected scripture verses. No response. She never moved. She never looked his way.

He turned around to leave feeling sad and empty, thinking he had failed. Then God put something on his heart. He turned around and said to her, "Before I go, I just want to say something God just put on my heart. Whatever you may have said, whatever you might have done, if you have confessed it to the Lord, whatever you might not be able to forget, He cannot remember."

And with those words she turned her head, looked at him, and started to cry and cry and cry. **Her memory of her actions had shamed her. Her thought of His memory of her actions had silenced her.**

"He forgave us all our sins, having canceled the written code…" (Colossians 2:14) The word canceled in the Greek means to wash out, wash away, or the wiping out of the memory of an experience. William Barclay comments, "Ancient ink had no acid in it" and "the ink could be wiped out as if it had never been." He then adds, "God, in His amazing mercy, banished the record of our sins so completely that it was as if it had never been, not a trace remained."

Maybe in heaven our sins are written on a dry erase board with a dry erase marker, and when confessed are wiped off the board as if they had never been. Confessed by us. Forgiven by Him. Forgotten by Him. Remembered no more by Him. Never revisited by Him.

The God of all creation, the God who created memory in us, chose "to remember our sins no more." But why? Why no memory of our confessed sins? Was it so He could love us more? Was it because we could love Him more? Or both? Or was it because He did not want the sins that shame us to also silence us?

Does His choice "to remember our sins no more" allow Him to love us to the fullest day after day, with no thought of yesterday's failures, yesterday's sins, or yesterday's pain we might have caused Him?

Can God receive greater **Glory** through us because He remembers our sins no more? Can God receive greater **Glory** through us because the sins He remembers no more will no longer weigh us down, thus allowing Him to be raised in greater **Glory**?

"He will wipe away every tear from their eyes." (Revelations 21:4)

Sometimes our sins bring a tear to our eyes. Sometimes our sins bring a tear to another's eyes. And sometimes, maybe our sins bring a tear to God's eyes.

But aren't you thankful that our God, who said in His word that He would wash away our sins and remember them no more, will one day in heaven wipe away our tears and our memory of those same sins? And all for His **Glory**.

His <u>Glory</u>. His dry erase board.

His Glory, His "Coming Home"

JOHN 17:18 "As you sent me into the world…"

JOHN 17:11 "I will remain in the world no longer, but they are still in the world, and I am coming to you."

JOHN 17:13 "I am coming to you now…"

JOHN 16:28 "I came from the Father and entered the world; now I am leaving the world and going back to the Father."

Have you ever seen the television show *Coming Home*? Stories of our brave soldiers coming home to the surprise of their loved ones. First the surprise, then the hugs and kisses, followed by the floodgate of tears of joy.

Our soldiers, leaving the comforts of home to protect our freedom.

Our soldiers, when duty calls, leaving their loved ones for their love of country. Our soldiers, willing to sacrifice their lives so we can live our lives.

Our soldiers, coming home after finishing the work they were sent to do.

A man, visiting a hospital where many of our soldiers had been taken to heal their wounds, came to a young soldier missing a leg. He asked him, "Son, how did you lose your leg?"

The young soldier replied, "Sir, in all due respect, I didn't lose my leg. I gave it while serving our country."

In John 10:11-18, Jesus uses the word "**lay**" five times:

V. 11 "The good shepherd **lays** down His life for the sheep."

V. 15 "... and I **lay** down My life for the sheep."

V. 17 "The reason my Father loves me is that I **lay** down my life."

V. 18 "No one takes it from me, but I **lay** it down… I have authority to **lay** it down."

Jesus **laid** down His life, it wasn't taken from Him.

Jesus gave His life, He didn't lose it.

Jesus left the comforts of Heaven to comfort us, His creation.

Jesus was sent by His Father, left heaven for earth, to exchange His **Glory** in heaven for His **Glory** on earth, that being a cross.

Jesus, willing to sacrifice His life so we could live our lives through Him here, and with Him there, that being Heaven.

ACTS 1:9 "AFTER HE SAID this, He was taken up before their very eyes and a cloud hid Him from their sight."

Jesus, sent by His Father in heaven, then laying down His life here on earth, and then taken up to His **Glory** that awaited Him in heaven. Leaving here, "coming home" there.

What was His coming home like in heaven? What do you think? What picture comes to mind?

Was it a private time of God the Father with God the Son? Just the two of them? Embracing in love? Talking with tears? Sharing with smiles?

Maybe a few of the old-timers there? Moses? Abraham? Isaac? Jacob? Joseph? Elijah? Isaiah?

And John the Baptist. Was he there with his head on tight and held high?

Or was there more? Were the final touches of His "coming home" celebration being made as Jesus was being led to the cross? And then, did heaven stand still as He was being nailed to the cross?

Was there total silence as all eyes were watching what was taking place at Calvary? Was there talk and prayers amongst the angels?

"Just six more hours, six more hours."

"God, please give Him strength."

"I can hardly bear to watch all that pain, all that suffering." "What love! What courage!"

"All those sins on one man, our Jesus."

"What a son! What a savior! What love!"

And then, when Jesus forgives those while on the cross and says, "It is finished," can you now hear all of heaven erupt with shouts of acclamation? Maybe a rolling thunder of applause throughout the streets of gold? Now listen to the angels.

"He did it!"

"Thirty-three years of perfection!" "To God be the Glory!"

"Jesus crucified, now Glorified!"

"In about 43 days, He's coming home!"

"Coming home in victory."

"Coming home to the Father."

Speaking of "coming home" to the Father, do you remember the story of the son who left for the far country in Luke 15? Do you think when Jesus talked about the "coming home" of that son to his loving Father, He had thoughts of His "coming home" to His loving Father?

Two sons. One in the story. One told the story.

Two sons. Both left their homes. Both left their fathers. One wanted to go. One was willing to go.

One left for sin. One left to die for sin.

Two sons. Both coming home. One after losing his wealth. One after laying down his life. One after coming to his senses. One after coming out of the tomb.

Two sons. One coming home to gladness. One coming home to **Glory**.

And then, after the confetti had been swept off the streets of gold, after the angels were catching their breath from their songs of praise and worship, after the trumpets had paused from their notes of adoration, after all the saints had bowed in thankful reverence, after all the tears of joy had fallen, and after the celebration of His coming home had ended, did he then go to work to prepare a place for you and me?

John 14:2 "I am going there to prepare a place for you." A place personally prepared by the master carpenter. Prepared by His hands. Hands still bearing the scars where spikes had been driven through His flesh. Prepared by His heart. The very heart of God, a heart willing to die here so we could have an eternal heart there.

In closing, our "coming home" there, to a place prepared by the hands and heart of God depends on if we have ever had a "coming in" time here. A time when we asked Jesus to forgive our sins, "come in" to our hearts, and be our Lord and Savior.

Are your hands now His hands? Is your heart now His heart?

Is the Lord now preparing a place for you in His **Glory**?

*His **Glory**. His coming home. Our coming home.*

51086192R00086

Made in the USA
San Bernardino, CA
13 July 2017